Aufklärung Catholicism 1780–1850

American Academy of Religion
Studies in Religion
edited by
Stephen D. Crites

Number 17
Aufklärung Catholicism 1780–1850:
Liturgical and Other Reforms in the Catholic Aufklärung
by Leonard Swidler

Aufklärung Catholicism 1780–1850

Liturgical and Other Reforms in the Catholic Aufklärung

Leonard Swidler

Scholars Press

Distributed by
Scholars Press
PO Box 5207
Missoula, Montana 59806

Aufklärung Catholicism 1780-1850:
Liturgical and Other Reforms in the Catholic Aufklärung

by
Leonard Swidler
Temple University

Library of Congress Cataloging in Publication Data
Swidler, Leonard J
    Aufklärung Catholicism, 1780-1850.

    (AAR studies in religion ; no. 17 ISSN 0084-6287)
    Includes bibliographical references.
    1. Catholic Church in Germany—History.
2. Liturgics—Catholic Church—History. I. Title.
II. Series: American Academy of Religion. AAR
studies in religion ; no. 17.
BX1536.S93   282'.43   78-2736
ISBN 0-89130-227-1

Printed in the United States of America

1   2   3   4   5   6

Edwards Brothers, Inc.
Ann Arbor, MI 48104

CONTENTS

INTRODUCTION

The word Enlightenment in the English speaking Catholic world, or Aufklärung in the German speaking Catholic world, has since the middle of the nineteenth century almost always had a derogatory connotation. The histories of the Catholic Church in Germany in the nineteenth century have usually depicted the Aufklärung as a cesspool of vice and have either denigrated or ignored the efforts of those German Roman Catholics who worked for reforms inspired by the Aufklärung during the first half of the nineteenth century. Even such a highly reputed Catholic historian as Franz Schnabel, writing in the 1930's, tended only to grant that Aufklärung Catholicism did contribute a few things to the welfare of the Church and was not so entirely black as it had been painted; but on the whole there was clearly more mischief than good there.[1] Aufklärung Catholicism was often pictured as rationalistic in the reductionist deist sense, as if it emphasized reason to the point of eliminating revelation; it was described as if it wished to destroy the institutional church, undermine all theology, corrupt morals and strip the liturgy of all meaning.

While it may be true to say these things of some thinkers, activists and perhaps even churchmen particularly in France, they are gross distortions, in fact countersigns, of the reality of most Aufklärung Catholicism in Germany. Aufklärung Catholicism was a reform Catholicism, and a reform movement, regardless of what those in power think at the time, is not out to destroy an institution but rather to re-form it; true, it may not be in a manner that is to the liking of those in power, probably because they would lose some of their personal power. But this is radically different from a movement which sets out to destroy an institution, as, for example, Communism attempts to destroy institutional religion.

In the area of theology Aufklärung Catholicism tried to lift what it saw as the dead hand of authoritarian dogmatism by putting what it thought was a rational basis under it all—an action it felt helped to promote rather than undermine theology. That Aufklärung Catholicism advocated some positions in theology which were later modified or rejected by ecumenical councils in doubtless true; that its opposition, including the official Catholic Magisterium, as in Pope Gregory XVI's *Mirari vos*, also suffered the same fate is also absolutely certain. (Compare it with the "Declaration of Religious Freedom" of Vatican II.) When the charge of the corruption of morals is pressed a little futher it turns out to be via the promotion of individual freedom and responsibility in things like religious freedom and freedom of speech. As for stripping the liturgy of form and meaning, Aufklärung Catholicism strove for, and often attained, the exact opposite; they wished to reform the liturgy to make it meaningful to the people.

A brief word must be said here about the use of the terms Aufklärung Catholicism in these pages. Although English scholars are accustomed to

1

using the term Enlightenment mainly in connection with the latter half of the eighteenth century, German scholars often find the reality of the Aufklärung running well into the first half of nineteenth century German history, and hence they frequently use the term Aufklärung to refer to pertinent persons and elements throughout that half of the nineteenth century. (Occasionally German scholars will refer to the Aufklärung in the nineteenth century as the late Enlightenment, *Spätaufklärung*, but more often they simply say Aufklärung.) The same is also true of the term Aufklärung Catholicism since the movement for the reform of Catholicism since the movement for the reform of Catholicism "in the light of reason," broadly understood, did not reach its high point till the 1830's, and made one last desperate attempt to survive in 1848.[2] A more descriptive term for this movement for reform in late eighteenth and early nineteenth century German Catholicism might be reform Catholicism. But in fact German scholars use that term, *Reformkatholizismus*, for the movement for Catholic reform at the *end* of the nineteenth century and refer to the earlier movement simply as the Aufklärung in Catholicism.[3]

When one digs through the anonymity and defamation of Aufklärung Catholicism a picture emerges that is extraordinarily similar to the Catholicism that arose over a century later from Vatican II (1962–65). But this latter Catholicism developed without any overt continuity with the former, which was reviled in its day by those who eventually triumphed over it. Even the memory of Aufklärung Catholicism and the reputations of its advocates have for the most part been obliterated, or, where that was not possible or desirable, distorted beyond all recognition by Catholic historians—and they were almost the only ones to write on the subject.

Although it is the first task of the historian to attempt to describe his subject as objectively as possible, "wie es eigentlich gewesen ist," analyzing and evaluating its various elements within its own context, such a properly executed task is by no means bereft of subjectivity. The very decision to undertake a specific task arises from within the historian as some kind of response to his contemporary context. This historical study was prompted by noticing how many of the positions approved and advocated at Vatican II seemed to resemble condemned positions attributed (albeit in very truncated fashion) to German Catholics of the first half of the nineteenth century. This observation naturally gave rise to the questions of what this earlier Catholicism really was like—as seen in the primary documents rather than through the filter of its enemies' descriptions—and secondarily how much it really was or was not like Vatican II Catholicism.

Research in the libraries of Southwestern Germany has proved extremely revealing; it is clear a non-tendentious history of the entirety of Aufklärung Catholicism awaits writing. It is as a step on the way toward the fulfilling of that task that this monograph dealing with the liturgical reforms of Aufklärung Catholicism has been written. Liturgical reform was chosen partly because it was such an important part of Aufklärung Catholicism and partly because the similarity between it and the contemporary liturgical reforms of Vatican II and afterwards was so striking that particular attention was drawn to it. This drawing of attention was intensified by the at times almost feverish concern of modern Catholic advocates of liturgical reform to disassociate themselves from the liturgical reform efforts of the early nineteenth century, of Aufklärung Catholicism.[4] One immediately wonders if "the gentleman doth protest too much." Hence, this study will concentrate on describing the liturgical reforms of Aufklärung Catholicism, but also when appropriate it will briefly compare those reforms with Vatican II reforms.

If the reforms of Aufklärung and Vatican II Catholicism are found to be substantially similar—which is the hypothesis—the implications will be manifold, not only for Catholic scholarship, and life, but also for the scholarship and life of those non-Catholics who come into significant contact with the Catholic Church, the largest Christian body in the world. One implication such a result would have for Catholic scholarship would be a further discrediting of that powerful authoritarian mentality that dominated Roman Catholicism for many generations until Vatican II: The Catholic Church in its authoritative structures does at times make what it later in practice recognizes as errors; basic commitments are made which are later reversed. Having historical documentation of such relativizes the old authoritarian claims. One implication such a result would have for non-Catholic scholarship would be to force it to take a more cautious, at times even sceptical, attitude toward descriptions of the "only acceptable" Catholic positions on various issues; the Catholic Church does reverse itself officially on basic issues—despite the most emphatic protestations.

The Historical Setting

Perhaps one of the most basic constitutive elements of the historical setting at the beginning of the nineteenth century lies over a century back, namely, the scientific revolution of the seventeenth century. The previous work of Copernicus, Kepler, Galilaeo and others found in a way a synthesis and culmination in the world-forming work of Sir Isaac Newton. As a result of Newton's work, and that of many other scientists, though supremely his, the world was seen as someting eminently *rational*. And because the world was rational in all of its parts all men and women needed to do to understand it was to study it diligently. They did not need to assume that they would never be able to solve the riddles of the universe; in fact, they should assume the opposite—look at Newton! Because the universe was essentially rational and because men and women were essentially rational, they had every hope and expectation of understanding the world. Then once they understood it they would be in a position to form and shape it in a manner that would most perfectly fulfill the world and, at the same time, naturally, be most beneficial to humanity—again, because both were essentially rational. Eighteenth century men and women, moreover, did not feel they came to this new, self-confident, optimistic world-view by some sort of leap of faith, for the Newtonian *Weltanschauung* of a rational universe was constantly proved anew and extended even by dozens and scores of amateur-scientists, throughout the eighteenth century; Benjamin Franklin and Thomas Jefferson are two famous examples in our own American history.

Doubtless just as basic a constitutive element of the historical setting of the beginning of the nineteenth century was the dynamic development in the economic sphere: the commercial and industrial revolutions. One does not need to be a Marxist to recognize the basic force of economics in history, although it was largely thanks to Karl Marx that the fundamental quality of this aspect of humanity's life was somewhat more properly focused on. For a long time in Western Civilization the dominant class was the aristocracy, lay and clerical, because they were the landholders, and land was the only really major source of wealth and power. However, the long development of the middle class from the medieval growth of towns, the burgeoning of trade in the Renaissance, and fantastic trade expansion in the age of discovery and colonialism, took an even greater leap forward with the coming of the Industrial Revolution, which began in England in the middle of the eighteenth century. As a result of the commercial and industrial revolutions the middle class was called into existence and, by the latter part of the eighteenth century, was catapulted into a position of great influence, and, as in the cases of the American and French revolutions, even of dominance.

However, while the industrial revolution tended to lift the middle class into power, it also initiated the Age of Masses. More and more peasants were drawn or driven from the land into the cities, or rather into the human swamps that formed around and in the cities. As business men and women and aristocrats with a business eye turned more and more land away from communal support to making an immediate monetary profit, more and more peasants could no longer exist in their ancestral villages. At the same time the same or similar business people were setting up factories in the cities which demanded manual laborers—cheap. Where in a society based on the land each individual had his and her own proper place and function in relation to all others, in the society based on commerce and industry a growing number of individuals became a part of a mass, with no specific proper place or proper function. However, this growth of a mass proletariat took place at different times in different countries; England was first, starting in the latter part of the eighteenth century. This Age of the Masses developed in many directions, such as in the beginnings of mass education, mass communications through the spread of literacy and the cheap newspaper, ever more rapid transportation, mass involvement in politics through the rise of democracy and socialism.

In the area of politics the dominance of the aristocracy was first curtailed or at least somewhat controlled by the monarchy, which became "absolute" in the sixteenth centuries, but which by the middle of the eighteenth century tended to be an "enlightened despotism." Here the new world-view of reason made itself felt, to some extent, through the enlightened prince, the modern version of Plato's philosopher king. One thinks preeminently of Frederick the Great of Prussia, Catherine the Great of Russia and Joseph II of Austria; but there were also many other "enlightened despots" of lesser fame in the latter part of the eighteenth century.

If reason was one key word that characterized the historical setting of the beginning of the nineteenth century, another key word was freedom. Freedom was sought in every sphere and it was heralded as the prime promoter of humanity's welfare, along with reason, its essential counterpart. In economics the move was away from the state's control through the mercantilistic system; in social and political affairs it was away from the dominance of aristocratic and royal priviliges; in thought and religion it was toward freedom from the tyranny of a stultifying authority and deadening tradition.

These two ideas, reason and freedom, burst into flames in 1789 with the French Revolution. Reason as an instrument of the "enlightened despot" was no longer considered a sufficient advance; reason had to become the instrument of all free men and women. But reason and freedom in many ways ran amuck during the Revolution; it ran into the tyranny of the Terror and later of the Tyrant, Napoleon. Still, even under Napoleon, and in many ways because of his genius, many economic, social, political and legal structures were "rationalized" and millions of men and women were liberated from a variety of oppressors. But the tyranny of France called forth, only very slowly at first, the resistance of an ever broader collection of men and women in the dominated lands. The form this resistance tended to take was that of nationalism.

Nationalism, as it developed in the nineteenth and twentieth centuries, is also a product of the Age of the Masses. It is hard to see how it could have developed in anything like the manner it did without an uprooted popular base, without mass education, communication, and transportation. Only with such building blocks could something beyond a provincial structure or a loyalty to a dynasty be erected. Nevertheless it was the French Revolution that fused all those elements, and others, into modern nationalism, first in France itself, and then in reaction to France's tyranny, in Germany, Italy and elsewhere.

One other major thing must be said about the general historical setting in Europe at the beginning of the nineteenth century: rationalism did not reign unchallenged; in fact, it called forth its antithesis, romanticism. Where rationalism stressed reason, logic, clarity, and reform on those bases, romanticism tended, among other things, to stress feeling, paradox, the mystical and, in Germany at any rate, reaction. However, the rise of romanticism was not like a light switch thrown on January 1, 1800. It had antecedents, particularly in Germany in the *Sturm und Drang* of the latter half of the eighteenth century, and the Enlightenment, the Aufklärung, continued to be a strong, though waning, force throughout much of the first half of the nineteenth century.

It is against this general European background that the reform efforts of the Catholics of the Aufklärung in Germany must be seen. In Germany itself it must be recalled that there was no unified state since the break-up of the empire of Charlamagne in the ninth century. There were actually hundreds of states in the Germanies at the beginning of the nineteenth century, which chaotic situation was changed by Napoleon during the first decade of the last century; he reduced the number of states to a dozen or so, all subservient to him. This political change drastically affected the Catholic Church in Germany since there were many ecclesiastical principalities, that is, states with archbishops, bishops or abbots as chiefs of state. These ecclesiastical states were almost entirely eliminated as ecclesiastical states; the land was turned over to secular princes, who were then beholden to Napoleon. Also huge numbers of abbeys, convents, churches etc. were secularized, that is, turned over to the state, which then sold or distributed them. But before the secularization took place there was a strong movement among German bishops to steer a course of relative independence vis a vis Rome, particularly exemplified by the efforts of Bishop Johann Nicholaus von Hontheim, the auxiliary bishop of Trier, who wrote his famous book in 1763 under the pen name of "Febronius," advocating greater episcopal power vis a vis Rome, much as the Gallicans were doing in France.

It should also be recalled that even in those German states which were not ecclesiastical principalities there was a tradition of union of church and state of one and a half millenia standing. The official church ever since the fourth century was in favor of this union, but always in the sense that the state would either be subservient to the church or at least would promote the welfare of the church as the official church understood that welfare, but certainly not in the sense that the state might undertake to reform the church. But it was exactly this latter effort that was made in the Austrian lands during the time of Maria Theresia (1740–80) and most particularly her son Joseph II (1780–90). It had a profound effect not only in the Austrian lands but also elsewhere, since it was often imitated. It is in this area of church-state relations that we will find the most glaring difference between Aufklärung Catholicism and Vatican II Catholicism.

1. LITURGICAL REFORM

On the first page of his history of the Liturgical Movement Dom Olivier Rousseau, OSB, states: "Let us understand that we are dealing with the true liturgical movement. . . . It has nothing in common, as we shall see, with a certain tendency of Jansenism and the Enlightenment, which at first sight it seems to resemble. The liturgical movement is, in fact, essentially opposed to such tendencies; for this reason, it has received the blessing of the Church. The 'liturgical reforms' of Jansenism and the Enlightenment were a part of the general breakdown of Christian thought and merely another expression of eighteenth-century laicism."[5] As noted, such an attitude toward the attempts of liturgical reform undertaken in the eighteenth century and the early nineteenth century is typical not only for most twentieth-century Catholic scholars[6] but also for all those who opposed liturgical reform in the period of the Enlightenment and subsequently. During the latter half of the seventeenth century Roman Catholics who promoted some kind of religious reform ran the serious risk of being categorized as Jansenist, which categorization, once Jansensim was condemned by Rome,[7] could be used as an effective weapon against them and their reforms. During the latter half of the eighteenth century and the first half of the nineteenth century a different constellation of motives and principles for liturgical reform became prominent, the Enlightenment, the Aufklärung. Because the Aufklärung was a vastly broader movement than Jansenism, whose very name indicates its personal origin, it could not so clearly be condemned by Rome. Nevertheless in the period of the Restoration, after the demise of the French Revolution, the term Aufklärung more and more became a weapon to be used against reforms and those who promoted them.

1. *Jansenist Inspired Reforms*

When Abbot Prosper Guéranger[8] began his liturgical studies and activities around 1830 he vigorously attacked the previous liturgical work and reforms of the seventeenth and eighteenth centuries as being Jansenistic, and therefore to be condemned.[9] However, Henri Bremond, in his famous work on religious literature in seventeenth-century France, saw much that was positive in the liturgical reform efforts of seventeenth-century French Catholics.[10] He found that there was a liturgical renaissance in France at this time that included an increase in liturgical studies, reform attempts in both the Missal and Breviary, and promotional efforts to bring the liturgy closer to the simple faithful.[11] One

7

example of this liturgical renaissance was the work of Nicolas Letourneaux, who, besides writing many articles, translated the Breviary into French[12] and produced the multi-volume *Année chrétienne*,[13] in which the Mass was translated into French. Because of this latter point the thirteen volumes were placed on the Index in 1695.[14] There had been a number of translations of the Mass into French before that time that did not draw such a penalty,[15] but the fear of Jansenism and its reform efforts changed the atmosphere drastically in the latter half of the seventeenth century, as can be seen from the fact that when in 1660 Josef de Voisin translated the Missal "according to the rules of the Council of Trent"along with an explication of the entire Mass, he was reproved by a very strong letter from Pope Alexander VII condemning such translations into the vernacular, because that would make the liturgy less holy and mysterious to the people.[16]

An interesting example of the sort of liturgical reforms that were promoted by Jansenists in the eighteenth century was related by Guéranger, with great disapproval, of course, for he ends the description with the statement that "such was the singular parade which the Jansenists conducted in the midst of France, by the grace of the tolerance of a lying archbishop [presumably Archbishop Noailles of Paris, d. 1729, who supported some Jansenist positions]." Guéranger's description is of Abbé Jacques Jubé, the Curé of Asnières. "Arriving at the foot of the altar he said the opening prayers, and the people answered in a loud voice. He next went to a chair on the epistle side of the sanctuary. Here he intoned the Gloria and Credo, without, however, reciting either of them through; nor did he say the Epistle or Gospel. He only said the Collect. He did not recite anything that the choir chanted. . . . They recited the formula aloud to show that their offering was being made in the name of the people. The entire Canon, as might be expected, was likewise recited aloud. The celebrant let the choir say the Sanctus and the Agnus Dei. . . . The communion of the people was not preceded by that of any of the ordained priests, as was the current custom. The subdeacon, although clothed in the tunic, communicated with the laity. Nevertheless the church of Asnières did not think it proper yet to use the vernacular in the liturgy. All that was done was that before vespers a sort of deaconess [sic—*une espèce de diaconesse*] publicly read the gospel of the day in French."[17]

The reform-orientation of Jansenism had a great deal of influence not only in seventeenth and eighteenth-century France, but also in the Austrian lands[18] and in northern Italy. This influence in a way reached a high point in the last two decades of the eighteenth century through the efforts of the two eldest sons of Empress Maria Theresia of Austria, Joseph and Leopold. Joseph, as the German Emperor, promoted far-reaching reforms throughout his lands north of the Alps. Leopold, as Grand Duke of Tuscany, did much the same in northern Italy, and for two years as Joseph's successor to the imperial throne. It was as a result of Leopold's encouragement that the diocesan synod of Pistoia in Tuscany was held in 1786, which, under the general influence of the Jansenist reform spirit, promoted a large number of religious reforms, including liturgical ones. The synod stated: that it wished to recall the liturgy "to a greater simplicity of rites, by expressing it in the vernacular language, by uttering it in a loud voice";[19] "that it is fitting, in accordance with the order of divine services and ancient custom, that there be only one altar in each Temple, [presumably so as to eliminate the possibility of simultaneous Masses] and therefore, that it is pleased to restore that custom."[20] These propositions, as well as many others, were condemned by Rome as being "rash, offensive to pious ears, insulting to the Church, favorable to the charges of heretics against it" in the first instance, and "rash, injurious to the very ancient pious custom flourishing and approved for these many centuries in the Church, especially in the Latin Church,"[21] in the second.

2. The Aufklärung

A more immediate influence than Jansenism, and in fact the matrix for Catholic liturgical reform efforts in the first part of the nineteenth century, was the Aufklärung. The Aufklärung of course began in the eighteenth century but it still was the most dynamic, dominant cultural force during the first part of the nineteenth century. The Aufklärung, which to a large extent came to Germany from France, nevertheless did not have the anti-religion or anti-church bias that it often did in France, partly because of the existence of the ecclesiastical states in Germany, for the leaders of the Catholic Aufklärung were often prince-bishops who utilized the services of reforming theologians and pastors.[22] Because the Aufklärung in Germany was relatively positive and reform-oriented it had an extraordinarily large influence on German Catholicism—vastly larger, and more beneficial, than is recognized today.

Of course not all Aufklärung Catholics took the same position on all matters; some were much more extreme than others. In fact, there was also naturally in some instances a wide variance in the positions held by the same men at different times in their lives. Johann Baptist Sailer (1751–1832), for example, was much more enthusiastic about the Aufklärung in the early part of his life than in the latter. This has been well known for quite some time— and accounts for the fact that he has been highly regarded by Catholics for a similar period of time.[23] The same of course is also true of Johann Adam Möhler (1796–1838), whose later work, *Symbolik* has been touted and hailed as his best, most mature, work (it is much more conservative than his earlier writings), whereas his first book, *Die Einheit in der Kirche* (much more liberal, non-papal, non-authoritarian) is often brushed aside as a work of his youth.[24] Only recently, however, has a somewhat similar movement to a more conservative position in older age been discerned in the writings of one of the most hated Aufklärer, Benedikt Maria Werkmeister.[25] Werkmeister, however, apparently did not move far enough to the right to be accepted by pre-Vatican II Catholicism. But even among those Aufklärung Catholics who are referred to as extreme[26] one does not find deist or Socinian positions held, although the charge has been made many times. At least this has been found to be the case where there has been objective research into the writings of the man, as, for example, Werkmeister.[27] Perhaps further evidence will come to light to show that Socinian ideas were held, for example, by some Catholic theologians at the University of Freiburg in the 1830's, as has been often claimed. But until the evidence is in hand one must be wary of the claims of the anti-Aufklärung people.[28] At any rate, what does seem clear is that even the so-called extreme Aufklärung Catholics were not anti-religious or anti-liturgical; they wanted very much to reform the religious life and the liturgical practice of their time.

Two other rather general misconceptions about the German Catholic Aufklärung should also be dealt with here in connection with liturgical reform. It is true that the Aufklärung placed great stress on reason, but it is not true that it did not also have an appreciation of feeling, a sense of beauty and a need to experience things. For example, Wessenberg,[29] doubtless the most defamed and execrated of the Aufklärung Catholics, was quite an able poet; he published scores of his poems during his lifetime. He was also deeply concerned that the ritual be reformed so that the faithful could have constant, creative religious experiences rather than the reenforcement of superstition, as was too often their usual liturgical fare. He sought a clear, simple beauty in the liturgy and worked hard to provide beautiful religious hymns for the worship services. Among Aufklärung Catholics there was not a lack of concern for feeling, beauty, and experience, but the understanding of these aspects of human life and their function in religion was doubtless different from that of the anti-Aufklärung Catholics. The same was also true in the case of the Aufklärung's stress on freedom, that is, Aufklärung Catholics did not therefore oppose rules and authority. In the matter of the liturgy they very much wanted rules, rules of reason, of historical continuity with the early Church, of pastoral effectiveness. They also very much wanted authority, in fact, they wanted even more authority, or rather, authorities, than before; only they wanted more and more people involved in the decision-making processes of the authorities. They were not anarchists, simply anti-authoritarians.[30]

There was a rather extraordinary interest in the liturgy and its reform on the part of Aufklärung Catholics. Waldemar Trapp lists eighteen different journals with an Aufklärung orientation, published for varying numbers of years from the 1780's to the 1850's, which ran articles on liturgical reform, a rather large number of journals for the relatively limited area of German-speaking Catholicism.[31] But Aufklärung Catholics saw the liturgy as an extremely important way to reach the lives of the masses of the Catholic faithful; they viewed the liturgy primarily in terms of a means to instruct and motivate the people. The concept that the liturgy also expresses humanity's relationship to God, i.e., worship, thanksgiving, penance, and petition, was not absent among Aufklärung Catholics, but they felt the stress on the instructional and motivational aspects of the liturgy was essential and sorely needed then.

3. *Mechanical Ritualism*

When Aufklärung Catholics observed the liturgical life around them they saw first and foremost an overwhelming mechanistic and spiritless performance of ritual. One liturgical scholar[32] saw this as a result of either a lack of understanding of what was being done or the constant repetition of the selfsame actions which tended to breed an "empty, spiritless mood."[33] Others stated, for example: "The frequent giving of blessings lessens their appreciation, as is the case with everything that comes up too often, and in the end they lose all impression on us. It is proper therefore that a blessing should be given most seldom, if it is to be an effective religious action."[34] This mechanical lifelessness was seen in such things as the almost constant use of the Rosary, the singing of Latin hymns and saying of Latin prayers by the people, who did not understand them, and the recitation of the Breviary insofar as it contained superstitious stories.[35] But perhaps the greatest concern was for the too often mechanistic performance of and attendance at Mass; the many movements and gestures performed by the priest and his assistants were seen to be often meaningless to the priest as well as the people, as were all the prayers, since they were in a foreign tongue.[36] Whatever the type of religious service, whether it was the Mass, administration of sacraments or sacramentals, or other devotions, the most frequent criticism voiced by Aufklärung Catholics was of mechanical, meaningless performance, so that Catholics became like "machines driven down the path of salvation."[37] So primary was this concern about a mechanical spirit in the liturgy that when the leading Aufklärung Catholic of the nineteenth century, Ignaz Heinrich von Wessenberg, became the Vicar General of the diocese of Constance he set up a series of prizes for the best books written on specified religious subjects; four of the first seven topics specified were liturgical, the first one being: "What means are most to be recommended to the pastor to overcome the mechanical spirit and luke-warmness of his congregation at religious services, especially in the hearing of holy Mass?"[38]

It was felt by many Aufklärung Catholics that one of the serious contributing factors to the mechanical spirit in the liturgy was the overstress on the teaching that grace flows automatically from rightly performed sacraments, i.e., the sacraments operate *ex opere operato*. The working of the sacraments *ex opere operato* was denied extremely rarely;[39] it was the disproportionate emphasis that was criticized. Franz Giftschütz wrote: "It is highly injurious and prejudicial to true devotion that so often the entire piety is built solely on the very frequent reception of the sacraments";[40] Dorsch and Blau complained that in the sacraments everything is *"opus operatum."*[41] Johann Theiner said that "all prayers are directed to having God *make* us good men. Everything is *opus operatum.*"[42] Vitus Anton Winter counter-suggested that all prayers be eliminated which "place man's entire hope in God and engender proportionately less self-responsibility on the part of man."[43] Even the quite moderate Johann Baptist Hirscher[44] complained bitterly about the overemphasis on *ex opere operato* "making the sacraments acts of magic" for the people.[45]

4. *Morality and Liturgy*

Aufklärung Catholics most of all wanted the liturgy to affect the lives of the people; liturgy had to issue in moral action to fulfill its purpose. They took very seriously the various biblical enjoinders that to love God one had to love neighbor: "Religion, according to reason and faith, is the same as the service of God [*Gottesdienst*, which is also the term used to designate "worship service"] and *Gottesdienst* is morality performed with a respectful consciousness of God." "The service of humanity [*Menschendienst*], performed with respectful consciousness of God, is worship [*Gottesdienst*]."[46] Though Aufklärung Catholics all stressed the overriding importance of morality in religion and liturgy, they were not all agreed on the basic philosophic orientation of this morality. One prominent orientation was that of Kantianism, which made the performance of duty the foundation of human life and viewed God as a judge who expected duty to be done for its own sake.[47] The second, and by far more prominent, orientation was what by its critics was usually called eudaemonism, i.e., what leads to true human fulfillment and welfare is the good, and therefore also authentic worship of God. The sacraments "are to be considered as means to foster the virtue and fulfillment of men, which constitutes the highest goal of the pastor."[48] However, this principle of seeking human fulfillment as the basis of morality was most often broadened by Aufklärung Catholics to mean the fulfillment of the whole human community. Bernard Bolzano,[49] for example, wrote: "From all your possible undertakings choose that one which, all consequences being considered, best promotes the welfare of the whole, regardless in which parts."[50]

5. *Instruction and Motivation*

The means whereby the liturgy was to promote morality was twofold: instruction and edification, or motivation. Often instruction was made primary, as when Vitus Winter stated that "the first goal of the liturgy is the religious moral enlightenment of the understanding";[51] "the second goal of external worship is the betterment of the heart, or edification."[52] He thought that everything about the liturgy should be made to serve moral doctrine: "Moral doctrine sounds from the chancel! The paintings on the walls of our temples proclaim moral doctrine! The statues on our altars proclaim moral doctrine! The ceremonies and observances in the holy Mass and administration of other mysteries all proclaim moral doctrine!"[53] But in another place Winter strikes a balance when he complains that too often "the entire effort is directed toward enlightening the mind, but leaves the heart untouched. . . . Therefore I have endeavored to show that the location of the religious principle is not to be sought simply in the understanding, but also, and preeminently, in the heart."[54]

An even greater emphasis on the motivational aspect of the liturgy was given by Sailer. He wrote: "General edification is the ultimate end of all devotional services,"[55] but elsewhere pointed out that "Man is more than just a head. . . . the most brilliant thought is still not an act of the will,"[56] and that "for an education of the understanding worthy of man, the education of the will is essentially and unavoidably necessary."[57] For Sailer "to make prayer merely a means to virtue and the liturgical leader merely a school teacher"[58] would destroy the liturgy, which should orient man toward God. Another example of the great number of Aufklärung Catholics who struck a balance in this central area of morality, religion and liturgy relationship, with a large variance in emphases, can be found in Bolzano. For Bolzano morality and religion are connected in the most intimate manner, but they are not identical; he strove to bring all the elements of Christianity, reason, revelation, worship and morality, into a system. In his system the sober, the useful, the welfare, not so much of the human individual, but of the human community, played a more prominent role, and the supernatural and mysterious a lesser role. He was like Sailer in balance, but unlike him in emphasis. Thus it was for the most part among Aufklärung Catholics.[59]

6. Preaching

A natural consequence of the Aufklärung's great concern for instruction and motivation in the liturgy was its envisioning preaching as an extremely important means to these ends.[60] Unfortunately, because of the Counter-reformation stress on the importance of the sacraments and the common notion that preaching was mainly a Protestant practice, and other factors, by the beginning of the nineteenth century preaching had become very infrequent among the Catholic clergy; in some areas many priests would preach no more than once a month, and then at a time when few people were likely to come.[61] Some Aufklärung Catholics, as a consequence, not only emphasized the importance of the sermon in the liturgy, but even spoke of it as the main thing. Werkmeister, for example, stated that "the most important function is the preaching office . . . not the office of the sacrificial priest or the Mass reader."[62] He often spoke "of the *duty* to listen to the sermon,"[63] while Winter complained: "why is one *commanded* to hear Mass, but only given a *recommendation* to hear the sermon?"[64] Of course, given the serious decline preaching had suffered within Catholicism it was quite natural that at least some reform Catholics stressed hyperbolically the importance of preaching. (In fact, that stance was also supported by Vatican II, for if the ignorance of the Gospel was as rife then as was claimed by Aufklärung Catholics, and there is ample evidence to support that contention, then the Church was faced with the missionary task of evangelization: Vatican II stated that "the *chief means* of this . . . [evangelization] is the *preaching* of the gospel of Jesus Christ."[65] Although not all Aufklärung Catholics spoke of preaching as the most important function, they all thought it essential and extremely important to the life of the Church.[66]

Despite all the accusations of their contemporary opponents and of subsequent Catholic scholars, Aufklärung Catholics really did not think of or utilize the sermons the way most Protestants did, and do, that is, most often in isolation from the Eucharist. They pleaded and worked for the fusion of the sermon and the Eucharist. Of course, they did not need to urge the encompassing of the sermon by the Eucharist, as do contemporary Protestant liturgical reformers, rather they needed to stress that "the priest will never celebrate the Holy Eucharist without a sermon, which should instruct the people concerning the mystery represented."[67] As Vicar General of the diocese of Constance Wessenberg found himself in a position to do something about what so many other Aufklärung Catholics could for the most part only write about: the uniting of the sermon with every Sunday Mass. On January 5, 1803, Wessenberg issued a circular to all the priests of his diocese requiring that at all Masses celebrated before noon on Sundays and major feast days a sermon be preached and in the afternoons Christian doctrine be taught; on the lesser feast days a choice between preaching and teaching was given.[68] Of course it was much more difficult to implement than to issue that order. Wessenberg did many long and short range things to see that it was carried out properly, including setting up regular clergy conferences, regional libraries for the clergy, a diocesan pastoral journal and constant written and personal contacts. Because the quality of the clergy was so low he felt impelled to also bring civil pressure to bear on the clergy. On February 12 of that same year he issued another order that the January 5th circular about preaching be read from the pulpit and that its reading be reported by the chief local civil official to the ecclesiastical deanery.[69] Such a technique, of course, was not at all uncommon at that time of union of church and state.

A closely connected point that might seem a little strange to present day American Catholics, but nevertheless urgently spoken of by Aufklärung Catholics very often, was that the "sermon should be preached after the gospel so that all the people might be present."[70] Although the sermon has almost always been preached at this juncture in the American Catholic tradition, it was often given before, after, or completely separately from the Mass in the European tradition until Vatican II. Aegidius Jais wrote that the sermon "should come after the gospel in the Mass, as it used to in the beginning,"[71] which Theiner supported by arguing that "the rubrics [in the Missal], the ancient church, and the nature of the case all require it."[72] As before, Wessenberg also acted on this issue. On March 16, 1809, he issued an order concerning worship services to the whole diocese of Constance: "The main parish worship service on all Sundays and required feastdays shall consist of a Mass [*Amte*] in the forenoon with German Mass hymns and a sermon, *which*

must take place during the Mass immediately after the first gospel . . . .
Likewise the Rosary may no longer be recited out loud during the parish Mass
or other morning Masses because, although the elements of the Rosary are
good in themselves, it is not suitable for a Mass devotion."[73] Resistance
against this order was also persistant, for Wessenberg was working against a
very comfortable custom whereby many avoided the sermon, which took
place most often, when it took place, before the Mass, by appearing at the
Church only at the beginning of the Mass (sometimes the end of the sermon
was announced by ringing the church bell!)[74] Nevertheless progress was made.

There were two different kinds of sermons that were advocated by
Aufklärung Catholics. Some, most often state officials, but not always, urged,
and sometimes commanded, that matters for the civil welfare of the
community be spoken of from the pulpit, things such as warnings against
quack practitioners, recommendation of vaccination, the latest information
on health practices, economic matters and agricultural practices.[75] At times
these matters may have been discussed from the pulpit without completely
absorbing the sermon time, but it is also doubtless true that there were times
when such topics constituted the entire sermon.[76] However, most Aufklärung
Catholics had a quite different, and more traditional, notion of what the
sermon should be. They thought first of all that the Scripture lessons should
be read aloud in German[77] and that the sermon should naturally then be an
explication of it, that is, the sermon should most often be a homily.[78]
Wessenberg again was in a position to do more than to write about and urge
the regular use of the homily; he issued many orders concerning its use to all
the priests of his diocese.[79] On March 31, 1803, he issued the following
ordinance: "that the priest who celebrates a morning Mass on Sunday or
feastday must always, after the first gospel, read the gospel of the day to the
people present and *give a quarter of an hour instruction on a text from it.*"[80]
All of this concern about the homily, of course, sprang from the great desire
on the part of most Aufklärung Catholics to spread the knowledge of the Bible
among the people,[81] which differentiated them quite distinctly from deists and
"rationalists."

7. The Vernacular in the Liturgy

Just like the Jansenist reformers before them, and the Protestant
reformers and the medieval reformers, and the liturgical reformers of the
twentieth century after them, Aufklärung Catholics came to the conclusion
that if the people were to participate meaningfully in the liturgy, the liturgy
would have to be celebrated in the language of the people. At the same time
the Jansenist-influenced Synod of Pistoia was advocating the use of a
vernacular liturgy[82] (1786), the German bishops gathered together at Ems
moved in a similar direction by advocating the use of German hymns at Mass
and Vespers.[83] This policy was put into action at least in the Austrian domain
already in 1782,[84] and in 1786 the Austrian government decreed that the

vernacular was to be used in the administration of the sacraments, particularly Baptism and Extreme Unction.[85] However, the 1782 recommendation of the commission for ecclesiastical affairs in Austria that the Mass be said in German was rejected by Emperor Joseph.[86]

Many individual theologians and churchmen also advocated in varying degrees the use of the vernacular in the liturgy. Johann Josef Nepomuk Pehem was one such theologian who in 1783 thought the "common people ought not stand around in the church like wooden statues."[87] "Would it not be most useful if the worship services were conducted and prayed in a language which the people understood and thereby fastened their attention on divine things, united their wills with the words of the priest and strengthened them with an inner anointing?"[88] Four years later Father Benedikt Peuger also recommended German hymns and worship services,[89] and two years after that Josef Anton Dorsch and Felix Anton Blau completely rejected the use of Latin in the liturgy.[90]

Aufklärung Catholics used many arguments for the introduction of the vernacular into the liturgy. In 1809 Friderich Brenner wrote the "language is the most useful and natural means to communicate to another perosn. . . . Language is the bond of all community. Nations divide themselves according to language—in the same way the servant of religion [the priest] places a divisive wall between him and the congregation present."[91] Most often support was drawn from St. Paul's First Letter to the Corinthians where Paul pointed out that in church speaking in a language other than the commonly understood one should be done only if there was an interpreter present: "Yet in the church I had rather speak five words with my understanding, that I may also instruct others, than ten thousand words in a foreign tongue."[92] Likewise frequently found were the questions: "The prayers of the Church are truly full of unction and power to lift up the spirit; therefore why should they not edify the people through an understandable presentation?"[93] "Why does one wish to withdraw from the faithful the stirring, strengthening qualities, so full of unction, which really are present in the Latin liturgy?"[94] But unfortunately the opposite often happened and certain superstitions were fostered by the veil of ignorance the Latin language spread,[95] whereas, "what a wonderful opportunity we had to bring to our people the best teachings from Holy Scripture . . . through the daily holy sacrifice of the Mass. That would really be the true means . . . to help dispel the generally obvious boredom which can be observed in our worship services."[96] It was also hoped that the use of the vernacular would help eliminate the spiritless celebration of the Mass all too frequent with priests, for "every priest would probably be ashamed of such an unworthy, detestable celebration if it had to be conducted in a language understandable to all the people."[97]

There were of course counter-arguments brought up against substituting the vernacular for Latin in the liturgy; these too were duly dealt with by Aufklärung Catholics. One argument for the retention of Latin was that the use of the vernacular would destroy the bond of unity with Rome; the response was that according to the will of the Apostle the bond of unity is not an incomprehensible language, but rather the same faith.[98] Another argument for Latin was that the changes in a living language could bring changes in the faith along with them—but despite this danger the Apostles did not write and preach in Sanskrit.[99] These arguments based on the advantages of a dead language were often brought up and in one instance inspired the exclamation: "Is there not an absolutely extraordinary ring to the statement: for the living presentation of religion a dead language is more suitable than a living one because the latter might in its development undergo several modifications! Through something dead, however, nothing living can be truly realized."[100] A corollary argument was also brought forth, namely, that if the liturgy were no longer in Latin priests would cease to learn Latin, and this would be a great loss; one response was, "Had Christ founded his religion to be a teaching exercise in a dead language among the people?"[101] Thus it was in general that Aufklärung Catholics dispatched the arguments against the use of the vernacular in the liturgy.

8. *Theologians in Favor of the Vernacular*

There were a number of theologians of major import in this period who expressed themselves more or less in favor of the use of the vernacular in the liturgy. Of these, four have enjoyed general favor with most conservative Catholic church historians subsequently. The first of these was Johann Baptist Sailer. His position, particularly later in life, was that of a moderate, but since he placed great importance on the participation of the people in the liturgy, he tended toward the use of the vernacular in the liturgy, particularly in the administration of the sacraments.[102] Nevertheless, he felt that the priest with the proper attitude and proper training could do a great deal to promote the participation of the laity in the Mass even when it was in Latin. He suggested such techniques as placing a translation of the Mass in the hands of the people and explaining it to them in school or elsewhere; having prayers read during Mass which would draw the attention of the people to what the priest was saying and doing; and he suggested a similar use of hymns during Mass.[103] Nevertheless he felt that the use of the vernacular in the Mass would be of great advantage: "If the German priests could one day celebrate worship service in the German language, oh then would the German word, enlivened by the basic mother language [for Sailer this meant the basic unspoken means of communication, that is, movement, posture, etc.] seize both the sensibility and the understanding, the reason and the emotions of the people at once, and the priest and the people would be One loving heart and One praying soul."[104]

The second of the four theologians, Franz Anton Staudenmaier,[105] also took a moderate position. Considering the use of the vernacular in liturgy he said: "We are far from wishing to draw the advantages of the Latin language into doubt. . . . All this, however, does not prevent allowing another language to take its place. . . . The employment of such a language might thereby become the means of bringing the priest and the people in the worship service into a truly inner and living unity."[106]

The last two theologians came from the Catholic Tübingen school. One, Johann Adam Möhler,[107] spoke out very early in his life and very strongly in favor of the vernacular in the liturgy. In reviewing a book he wrote: "Thus we must stand astonished how someone could arrive at the thought that an un-understandable foreign language could serve to edify the people! Doesn't the language given by God to every people serve them in all circumstances of life? Why, therefore, not for us in exactly that place where this divine gift could be put to its most beautiful use, namely, in the communication of religious sentiments in the solemn acts of our entire liturgy!"[108] Möhler then went on to give a brief history of the development of the liturgical language and the vernacular in Western Europe. At the end of this history he concluded: "Nevertheless, after the natural reasons for retaining the Latin language in the liturgy no longer had any force, other reasons were put forth, so that now, although there were really no longer solid reasons, it was made to appear that there were. Just listen to the reasons which the author puts forth: 1. In a large building, he says, one would nevertheless not be generally understood. (Therefore, because here and there a German liturgy might not be understood throughout the entire church, a language should be retained which would be understood in no place!) 2. The author points to the ancient dignity of the Latin language. (Should one not rather choose Hebrew; this is much older yet?) 3. He is in favor of the retention of Latin for the sake of uniformity, and according to page 22, because it is a becoming symbol of church unity. (But our unity consists in doctrine, in the essential acts of worship, and in the structure laid down by Christ. . . . What a wonderful unity when no congregation in the entire Catholic world understands its priest! Uniformity alone can never be a reason for the introduction of any matter . . . for could it not also be a uniformity in foolishness?)"[109]

Two years later Möhler wrote an article on Catholic missions, and among other things, insisted that pagans not be burdened with a Latin rite, as had been the case. He felt that if any worship service in the vernacular was desirable among German Catholics (and it was), that it was even more desirable and necessary among the pagans, who did not grow up in Christianity and absorb many of its teachings through various means, such as schooling and so on. He also argued that it was a terrible waste of time and effort to have the pagan children spend so much of their time studying Latin when there were so many who needed to learn about the essentials of Christianity. [110]

The fourth German Catholic theologian of the first half of the nineteenth century who is still quite well known today and who also came out very strongly in favor of the vernacular in the liturgy is Johann Baptist von Hirscher. Father Hirscher began his university career at the University of Tübingen when it first established its Catholic theological faculty. Shortly thereafter, in 1821, Prof. Hirscher published in Latin a book on the reform of the Mass.[111] Among the many suggestions for the reform of the Mass Hirscher recommended celebrating the Mass entirely in the vernacular language.[112] Although Hirscher was convinced that the use of the vernacular was an absolute necessity, he did not believe that its use was sufficient to adequately reform the celebration of the Mass.[113] He felt a whole series of reforms needed to be implemented so that the priest would be, among other things, placed among the people, facing them and in an effectual dialogue with them during the celebration of the Mass.[114] Unfortunately, within two years this work of Hirshcer's was placed on the Index. As a consequence Hirscher began to be somewhat more cautious. For example, in later writings he was at pains to point out all the reasons which argued in favor of the retention of Latin, or at least the legitimation of its use, in the liturgy; he did this even up to twenty-five years after his first book on the reform of the Mass, in a multi-volume work on the religious problems of the day.[115] However, even here Hirscher was careful to indicate "the Council of Trent has not pronounced the living language of any country inadmissable altogether, as in so doing she would convict herself in allowing the use of the Greek liturgy. The Council has merely proposed to settle the point, that it did not seem convenient *ut Missa vulgari passim lingua celebratur*. Its anathema, therefore, applies only to the case of those who assert, absolutely, '*lingua tantum vulgari Missam celebrari debere.*' Canon ix, session xxii."[116]

Two years after this last statement was written, the situation in Germany, as in most of Europe, changed drastically with the revolutions of 1848. As a consequence of the changed situation Hirscher was encouraged to strike a blow in favor of a whole series of reforms, the keystone of which was the establishment of diocesan synods which would take up and promote the other reforms. To this end he published a book in 1849, while the Revolution was still *in via*, which quickly went through three printings and was translated into both French and English.[117] In this book Hirscher admitted that he had up to very recently written about the various reasons supporting the use of Latin in the liturgy, but went on to state: "But I have not denied, that the *genuine idea of worship*, as a public and common act for common edification, *can only be fully realized by the employment of the vulgar tongue*. But this too is a matter which must and will demand the attention of the Church in synod, and the laity will give a decisive voice in its favor."[118] Hirscher also produced other arguments for the use of the vernacular, which were quite reminiscent of his 1821 work. For example, he wrote: "Others, chiefly the common people, who are sufficiently content with their Latin services, feel themselves thus satisfied rather from the force of habit, than from the supply of their spiritual wants. How edifying, for example, are the solemnites of Holy Week! Is it not lamentable that the people cannot have a part in them? Or, is it a good sign, if they are perfectly contented to be merely lookers-on in such services? The common folk have become indifferent to worship, according to the existing service, inasmuch as they are not partakers in it."[119] Again, Hirscher pointed out that the use of the vernacular, essential as it was, was not sufficient by itself. "But in case the laity should evince this creditable desire for a part in divine service, for common offices, and for common prayer, and above all for a worship celebrated in the mother tongue, it will be all important to avoid mere half measures. Simply to translate the Latin liturgy, will not suffice. Much of it is indeed surpassingly good, but not all. . . . Another half measure would retain the Canon in the Latin tongue, allowing the priest to sing in the language of the worshippers such parts as the Gloria, the Collects, the Gospel, and Proper Preface. But what will this amount to? Something much more thorough must be done, or the whole should be let alone."[120] Unfortunately, this work of Hirscher was also placed on the Index on October 25, 1849. Hirscher, shortly thereafter, submitted to Rome; the Revolution in Germany, as well as France, was defeated and all of the great hopes for reform were obliterated.

9. Churchmen in Favor of the Vernacular

Not all priests were content with merely advocating the use of the vernacular in the liturgy. It is difficult, of course, to ascertain just how many did use the vernacular and to what extent. However, there is even documentary proof that some did use the vernacular in the liturgy. One such priest for whom there is documented proof is Anton Selmar of Bavaria.[121] According to his own testimony in his parish archives, Selmar conducted baptisms, marriages and funerals in German,[122] and when he was a pastor of Berg by Landshut he "conducted with dignity in the German language Holy Communion, Baptisms, marriages, funerals, processions, prayer hours—readings, hymns, psalms, meditations, and prayers."[123]

Another such activist priest was Father Beda Pracher from the upper Palatinate.[124] In 1806 Pracher published a Ritual in which it was indicated that the various parts of the Mass which the priest began out loud, such as the Gloria and the Creed, were to be spoken or sung in German by the priest. The priest was also to read the Epistle and Gospel in German after he had read it quietly in Latin, first.[125] On page 12 of this Ritual, Pracher wrote that his diocesan chancery office had already given permission to a number of pastors to celebrate several portions of the Mass in German. It was on the basis of this, apparently, that Pracher formulated his general principle that whatever was to be read or sung out loud, was to be read or sung in German.[126] In 1836 Pracher's Ritual was still used in the town of Thalheim, and eleven years earlier, in the town of Imnau, the pastor remarked: "The Mass (on Good Friday) was celebrated according to Pracher's prayer book entirely in German, so that not a single Latin syllable was heard. . . . This worship service enjoyed a most enthusiastic reception."[127]

The most influential of the early Aufklärung Catholics promoting the use of the vernacular in the liturgy was doubtless Father Benedict Maria Werkmeister, who in 1784 became a court preacher at Stuttgart. There he was largely responsible for convincing the Duke to have Matins and Lauds of

Holy Week translated into German.[128] In the same year, Werkmeister published a hymn and a prayer book for use in the Stuttgart court chapel.[129] He stated there: "Attempts have been made to help the people by means of prayer books, but more has been done thereby to promote silent devotion than communal and public prayer in which the priest and the people join together in one voice."[130] Werkmeister, however, did not stop with Matins and Lauds or hymns. He proceeded to put into German parts of the Mass; first of all, the Epistle and the Gospel and the Orate Frates, and then later the Gloria, Credo, Suscipiat, Dominus Vobiscum, Sanctus, Pater Noster, Agnus Dei, Domine non sum dignus. The Canon however was left untouched in Latin.[131] Werkmeister expressed in words his experiences in the use of the vernacular in a work on the German Mass at the court chapel in Stuttgart, published in 1787.[132] Here he advocated the general introduction of German into the liturgy, giving both many of the reasons already recorded above and also the argument that the various national characters found the natural expression of their varying patterns of thought and feeling in their own language; therefore, each nation ought to have its liturgy in its own language.[133] In 1789 Werkmeister published another work promoting the use of the vernacular in the liturgy.[134] Here again he argued that, "It is a characteristic mark of every good liturgy that it unite the laity present with each other and with the priest; in houses of prayer all the gathered Christians must be only one moral person. . . . Why do we not grasp the simplest, most satisfactory, most straightforward, and only, means to obviate all the difficulties—a liturgy in the vernacular?"[135] With such a record of writing and acting in favor of the vernacular in the liturgy, it is easy to see why the conservative Catholic historian Sägmüller not only referred to Werkmeister's efforts as the beginning of the "German Mass" but also attacked him vigorously as an *Aufklärer*.[136]

As we have already seen, one of the most important Aufklärung Catholics was Ignaz Heinrich von Wessenberg, who was able not only to promote ideas by writing and put them into action for himself, but as administrator of the diocese of Constance was able to effectively put many liturgical reforms into action throughout the southwestern portion of Germany and most of German-speaking Switzerland. Concerning the use of German in the liturgy it should be noted first of all that Wessenberg did *not* promote the German Mass; he even took steps against those priests who did presume to celebrate the Mass in German in his diocese. What he did do in the Mass was to prescribe that the Scripture lessons be read in German after they had been silently read in Latin by the priest; he also promoted the use of German hymns during the Mass.[137] It was in 1809 that he decreed that German hymns were to be sung at all communal Masses.[138] Three years later the diocese of Constance itself put out a hymn and prayer book to be used during worship services; Wessenberg himself contributed a number of hymns and free translations of the Psalms to this hymn book.[139]

However, already in 1805 we find that Wessenberg moved in the direction of promoting the use of the vernacular in portions of the liturgy other than the Mass. One of the questions that the pastors had to answer in a questionnaire was whether or not Vespers was celebrated on Sundays and Feast Days and whether or not they were sung in German.[140] By 1809 Wessenberg was insisting on the celebration of public Vespers in German so that the people might participate, a custom which has continued in the diocese of Freiburg and Rottenburg down to the present time.[141] As was noted before, Wessenberg encouraged the priests of his diocese to think seriously about various kinds of improvements that they could suggest and offered prizes for the best written catechisms, essays on specific subjects, etc. This encouragement also included urging his priests to write various translations and reformulations of formularies for the administration of sacraments—in German, of course. The results were manifold, including, for example, a baptismal rite for when a Catholic priest had to baptize children of Protestant parents,[142] and a wedding rite for when a Catholic priest had to bless the marriage of a couple when one or both of the parties were non-Catholic Christians.[143] Wessenberg also very early insisted upon the use of German in such public liturgical functions as the procession on Ash Wednesday and also on the feast of Corpus Christi.[144] As more and more of the sacraments and sacramentals were ordered to be conducted in German, the requests piled up for Wessenberg to publish a new Ritual. However, because Wessenberg was reluctant to proceed too hastily in such matters of reform, the myth to the contrary notwithstanding, it was not until some four years after he had been forced out of public ecclesiastical office that he ventured to publish his Ritual, in German.[145]

In this matter of an energetic but somewhat moderate employment of the vernacular in the liturgy, as in his other reforms, Wessenberg met with some persistent resistance. For example, on the 25th of May 1820, Wessenberg felt compelled to send a decree to the Deanery of Veringen complaining that in eight specific parishes the public Sunday Vespers were still celebrated in Latin (although in one of the parishes they had been celebrated in German under the previous pastor) and that in three particular parishes the Gospels and prayers during the Ash Wednesday ceremonies were also still read in Latin; the pastors were requested forthwith to conduct these services in German.[146] Over a year later Wessenberg was still having difficulties in the same area, as is indicated by his decree of October 11, 1821, where he emphatically insisted: "1. The sermon will uniformly be delivered during the Mass immediately after the Gospel; 2. That the still persisting custom of conducting Vespers in Latin, which is spiritually unrewarding for the people, be discontinued, according to the earlier directives."[147] Despite these resistances to the employment of the vernacular in Wessenberg's jurisdiction (they were, relatively speaking, really surprisingly few), it is clear that Wessenberg doubtless did more than anyone else to spread the use of the vernacular in the liturgy in Germany, the influences of which have lasted to the present.

The work of reforming the liturgy was in some ways continued and spread further in southwestern Germany in the diocese of Rottenburg, which was set up in 1821 by the Papal Bull *Provida sollersque*; it was formed from sections of various other dioceses, including that of Constance. The first Bishop of the diocese of Rottenburg was Johann Baptist von Keller.[148] On July 5, 1837, Bishop Keller issued a general regulation for worship services in the diocese of Rottenburg.[149] Keller continued much of the same use of the vernacular in the liturgy that Wessenberg had. For example, he required that during the Sunday Mass German hymns be sung,[150] and on Sunday afternoons after the period of Christian doctrine was finished, German Vespers were to be conducted.[151] To this end Keller had published in the following year a Catholic hymn and prayer book for the public celebration of worship services in the diocese of Rottenburg which contained many German hymns and prayers for the Mass and Vespers.[152] In his 1837 decree Bishop Keller, in speaking of the need for a new, unified diocesan Ritual for the administration of the sacraments, stated that the "use of the mother tongue in the administration of holy sacraments and several other ecclesiastical activities is becoming more and more a pressing need in our time."[153]

The reaction to Bishop Keller's 1837 regulation for worship services was, of course, mixed. For example, there was a very favorable response from a number of the priests of the neighboring diocese, Baden.[154] On the other hand, an extremely negative response was published in the very conservative Catholic magazine *Katholik*.[155] The anonymous author had, among other biting criticisms, the following remarks to make concerning Bishop Keller's statement that the use of the vernacular in the liturgy was a pressing need of the times. "It is the pressing need of some unchurchly priests, particularly in the Baden and Württemberg areas, who are always speaking of this pet theme of theirs because only thereby can they hope to cause a stir and because they wish to reform everything—except themselves. What is a pressing need of our time is that the people, but even more, the clergy, become more pious and zealous and exchange their earthly mentality for a heavenly one that the people and the clergy again return to God. It is questionable whether this can be accomplished more by a German worship service than through the Latin one used up until now. Experience speaks not at all in favor of the former. Rather, eye witnesses have with pain reported very sad tales of the scandal, the luke-warmness, the coldness, the church-shyness to which unchurchly priests have condemned some places with their German-enthusiasm. If the use of the mother tongue in the worship service were a pressing need of our time, we would not hear of this need merely here and there, in a corner of the earth exactly where an unchurchly spirit resides, but rather, everywhere, in Italy, France, Belgium, Austria, Bavaria, in short, in all Catholic lands. Also, the people, whose tact is often far more correct than the tact of some clergy, would not be expressing their opposition to it. Also, Rome, the center of unity, which is obliged to care for the entire church, and which also surely knows its need best of all, would certainly have long since been aware of such a need and would have taken care of it."[156] Then, in an interesting *post hoc, ergo propter hoc* line of reasoning the author continued: "We see an unavoidable consequence among the Protestants who already three hundred years ago introduced the mother tongue. Their churches stand empty, reverence is driven from them. Our churches also would soon meet the same fate if piety were to be sustained only by the German language! . . . Oh, do not wish to be wiser than the mother of all believers who is ruled by the Holy Spirit. The worthy veteran Geiger, who already so often hit the nail on the head, said in this regard (*Sion*, May, No. 64), 'what these progressive gentlemen find least of all to their taste and what they particularly loudly demand must be changed is the Latin language in the worship service; perhaps in order to relegate to oblivion the Latin Church, which alone in this and every time sustains Christianity?'"[157]

Brief mention here might also be made of another Catholic priest of southwestern Germany who also vigorously promoted the vernacular in the liturgy, Father Fridolin Huber.[158] Huber strongly supported the reform efforts of Wessenberg and Bishop Keller, including of course, the use of the vernacular in the liturgy. Huber supported the use of the vernacular because he felt that anything not understandable in prayer was both senseless and contrary to the purpose of prayer, and because for him the liturgical ideal was that of the communal prayer performed by the people and the priest together.[159] On the contrary, he saw the use of the Latin language in the Mass and the administration of the sacraments as a divisive wall between the people and the clergy.[160] He also argued that the use of the vernacular was basically biblical, since that is what Christ used at the Last Supper.[161] Concerning the total use of the vernacular in the Mass he was for awhile ambivalent, as indicated by the fact that in 1825 he spoke in favor of putting the Mass entirely in the vernacular,[162] and in 1826 he indicated that he thought conducting the Mass in the vernacular was not necessary because the text in translation could be put into the hands of the people.[163] Nevertheless he did eventually decide in favor of conducting the Mass in German, which position was expressed in an article in 1838 supporting the liturgical reforms of Bishop Keller, and suggesting a number of expansions, including that of placing all of the Mass in German.[164]

There was at least one other significant force in German Catholicism which promoted the use of the vernacular in the liturgy—that was the synodal movement, which, though in some ways begun back in the period immediately after the 1815 Congress of Vienna, rose to its greatest strength in the years between 1830 and 1849.[165] Various Aufklärung Catholics referred in different ways to the need for the synod to take up the question of the vernacular in the liturgy. One, for example, was Wessenberg who, when in 1831 he published his German Ritual, stated in his expanded title that this work was one which "was to be placed for testing before the Most Reverend Archbishop and Bishops . . . and the forthcoming synods to be held by them." In 1834 and 1836 in articles on what should be discussed in diocesan synods the use of the vernacular was included,[166] as was also the case in the book published by Johann Baptist von Hirscher in 1849 on the holding of synods.[167] A similar concern for the use of the vernacular in the liturgy was expressed by Father Frantisek Nahlovsky, who called a meeting of many of the leading clergy in the area around Prague, Czechoslovakia, in order to support the establishment of a number of reforms and the calling of a diocesan synod to which these reforms would be submitted including, of course, the use of the vernacular.[168] In general, it could be said that all those in favor of a diocesan synod were also in favor of the employment of the vernacular in the liturgy. It should also be noted that the examples given here are only a portion of those Aufklärung Catholics who expressed themselves in favor of the use of the vernacular in liturgy; of course the number of those who did not express themselves in writing in favor of the use of the vernacular would naturally be far greater.

10. Reaction Against the Vernacular

Effective efforts to curb the use of the vernacular in the liturgy in southwestern Germany began in the diocese of Freiburg particularly in the middle and late 1830's. For example, a Freiburg diocesan Ritual was published[169] which, although it used a considerable amount of German, in many instances taken directly from Wessenberg's Ritual, nevertheless employed a good deal more Latin than did Wessenberg's Ritual of 1831. Rösch reports a number of pastors' reluctance to give up the use of the Wessenberg Ritual for the more Latinate Freiburg Ritual.[170] As early as the year 1850, even in the area immediately around Constance, which was most supportive of the Wessenberg, it was reported that the High Mass was sung entirely in Latin by the priests of the entire area.[171] Thus, although a number of features of the reforms making use of the vernacular in the liturgy persisted into the twentieth century when the Liturgical Movement took up the cause of the vernacular again, most of the use of the vernacular in the liturgy was either eliminated or drastically reduced by the middle of the nineteenth century.[172]

11. Aufklärung Stress on Community

Use of the vernacular promoted not only understanding on the part of the people, which Aufklärung Catholics very much desired, but it also helped to forge another element which Aufklärung Catholics greatly desired, namely, community. In the usual stereotype of the Enlightenment, or Aufklärung, one does not normally expect to find a stress on community; this is a characteristic usually reserved for the anti-Aufklärung movement, Romanticism. But, contrary to stereotyped expectations, one finds among Aufklärung Catholics a great deal of concern for the building of community, and particularly by way of the liturgy. For example, Johann Baptist von Hirscher in 1821 wrote that the true ideal of the celebration of the Mass can be attained only if the people really participate in it, if a unity develops between the people and the priest.[173] Johannes Theiner expressed much the same ideal a decade later when he wrote that, "The priest and the people must pray together in communal fashion."[174] Stress was consequently placed on the priority of the communal celebration of the liturgy over private prayer and popular devotions, much as also occurred in the twentieth century Liturgical Movement.[175] One Aufklärung theologian even argued that the hearing of a private Mass on Sunday was insufficient to fulfill one's Sunday obligation, but that this obligation bound one to attentively participate in a community Mass, indeed, perhaps even the parish community Mass.[176] Another way the stress on community in the liturgy expressed itself was by the insistence that, "Never should a holy Mass be celebrated except that at the same time the priest communicates, several of the faithful likewise communicate."[177]

12. *The Multiplicity of Masses*

In striving for a development of community Aufklärung Catholics saw as important not only how the Mass was said but also where and when and how often. They were particularly disturbed by the practice of having more than one Mass being said in the same church simultaneously (which, of course, any Roman Catholic born before 1964 will also remember). Already under the leadership of Emperor Joseph II of Austria this custom was attacked vigorously when on February 25, 1783, a Viennese state police order was issued forbidding the simultaneous celebration of several Masses, allowing them to be said only in sequence and solely at the high altar.[178] The worship service order for Munich on October 27, 1827, referred to this Austrian ordinance and also required a similar observance.[179] Early in the nineteenth century men like Wessenberg moved to eliminate the celebration of simultaneous Masses, particularly on Sundays.[180] About the same time Brenner bitterly complained, "For over twelve hundred years no other Mass took place simultaneously alongside the general parish Mass. . . . Now during the High Mass manifold private Masses are said, to the serious downgrading of the former."[181] Shortly thereafter Johann Baptist von Hirscher also entered the lists against the celebrating of simultaneous Masses, which disturbed the unity of the community.[182] Bishop Keller of Rottenburg included a similar proscription in his 1837 worship service ordinance: "During the parish main worship service another private Mass may never be celebrated."[183] Bishop Keller also extended that principle to state that with certain exceptions "Outside of the parish church on Sundays and Holy Days in no other church . . . may a Mass be celebrated or any other worship service conducted, and such non-parish churches should be closed during the celebration of the parish Mass."[184]

It was not just the celebrating simultaneously of more than one Mass in the same Church that disturbed the Aufklärung Catholics. They were very aware of what the Viennese Court Chancery referred to as "The custom of having a

Mass being celebrated at whatever time one enters a church which has become almost a religious necessity, especially in the large cities. . . . To the extent that this necessity increases the priestly caste, to the same extent does the reverence due to the holy Mass decrease and also the correspondence with the practice of the early Church."[185] As a consequence of the growth of this attitude Aufklärung Catholics began to express their opposition to private Masses. One example is found in an article from 1802 where the author stated that, "I have no hesitation in freely asserting that such private Masses, which in their manner of celebration completely contradict the manner in which the Apostles celebrated the Holy Supper, are destructive."[186] Shortly thereafter more Catholic authors joined the chorus against the celebration of private Masses. The positions taken ranged from that of Anton Winter who argued that the private Mass contradicted the ideal of the community worship service,[187] to that of Anton Selmar, who opposed entirely the celebration of any private Masses.[188] The opposition to private Masses was continued by Friderich Brenner, who also viewed private Masses as being destructive of the public communal worship service,[189] and still later by Johann Baptist von Hirscher, who urged that the celebration of private Masses be avoided.[190] Such opposition to private Masses was given additional encouragement in 1837 by Bishop Keller, who in his worship service ordinance did not completely forbid private Masses, but severely restricted them: "After the parish Mass no further private Masses may be celebrated."[191] This stand on private Masses, of course, added fuel to the charges leveled by the anti-Aufklärung Catholics that the Aufklärung Catholics were Protestantizing the Church, the argument being one of guilt by association.

Of course, if priests followed the recommendations of these Aufklärung Catholics and avoided celebrating private Masses there would then not infrequently be occasions when priests would not have congregations for whom to celebrate Mass. Aufklärung Catholic theologians were naturally aware of this and therefore made suggestions like the following: "In cities or other places where there are several priests they should, instead of celebrating Mass for themselves, attend the parish Mass and . . . receive the Eucharist from the hands of the celebrant of the Mass."[192] As a consequence many priests, especially in southwestern Germany, gave up the custom of celebrating Mass themselves every day since in their situation they did not always have a congregation.[193]

13. Eucharistic Reforms

Aufklärung Catholics felt that one of the essential ways in which the communal aspect of the Mass had to be manifested was by the receiving of Holy Communion, not only by the priest, but also the laity present. Already in the latter part of the eighteenth century one German Catholic theologian wrote that, "At public worship all those present should also receive communion together."[194] Then in the first part of the nineteenth century, when the Aufklärung liturgical reform movement grew stronger, Vitus Anton Winter began to call for a return to the practice of primitive Christianity, where both the priest and the laity communicated at the same time.[195] Around the same time, Benedikt Peuger went so far as to write: "A Mass should never be celebrated in which at least several of the faithful do not communicate along with the priest."[196] In 1821 Johann Baptist von Hirscher wrote something quite similar when he insisted that, "There should be no Sunday or feast day Masses which lack communicants."[197] But Hirscher also went further when, like Vitus Anton Winter, he called for a return to the practice of the early Church, where *everyone* in the congregation received the Eucharist: "Therefore the ancient Church knew nothing of a Mass without general communion, and nothing of communion except during the Mass."[198] Wessenberg, as usual, was in a position not to just write about a reform; he also put his weight as diocesan administrator behind it. Thus, for example, in his Ritual he not only pointed out that the Council of Trent recommended that the laity receive communion during the Mass, but also urged a *general* reception of communion, and when this was not forthcoming, that at least several of the faithful be encouraged to come forward.[199] Even the great Johann Adam Möhler, in moving from his more liberal first book, *The Unity in the Church*, published in 1825, to his more conservative work, *Symbolism*, published in 1832, supported the notion of a general communion by all of the faithful at the Mass: "The bad situation whereby on Sundays the whole community no longer communicates, as in the early Church, but the priest normally alone receives the body of the Lord in the Mass, is not to be laid at the feet of the Church, since all of the prayers of the sacred ceremonies presume a real communion by the entire congregation."[200]

In connecting the stress on the notion of community with the celebration of the liturgy, and primarily the Mass, Aufklärung theologians not only tended to conclude that the laity, most often the entire congregation, should, as well as the priest, communicate at Mass, but also that the Eucharist itself was essentially a social sacrament. Therefore, communion should normally be given only *during* the Mass, the communal celebration of the Eucharist. This attitude, for example, was somewhat adumbrated in the quotation just given from Möhler. It was rather more clearly put forth in the 1821 work of Hirscher: "Therefore the ancient Church knew nothing . . . of communion except during the Mass."[201] Later, however, Hirscher, under the pressure of the indexing of his book and a general conservative reaction, retrenched his position somewhat and defended the custom of distributing communion outside of the Mass, although he still maintained that the ancient custom of distributing it during the Mass was the better one.[202] Wessenberg also drew the logical conclusion from his stand that the laity should all receive communion along with the priest during Mass and thereby wrote: "The reception of Holy Communion outside of holy Mass is a custom which fits very little in the spirit of the Church."[203] Much the same thing was also said by the theologian Karl Schwarzel: "Likewise concerning the present-day manner of receiving communion it should be noted that the custom of receiving communion outside of or after the Mass is an abuse."[204] A close corollary to the proposition that in order to stress the communal aspect of the Eucharist Holy Communion should normally be distributed only within the celebration of the Mass is the notion that wherever possible the hosts distributed during communion be consecrated at the same Mass.[205] This, of course, was a practice that has been rather atypical in traditional Roman Catholicism, but which was advocated more and more vigorously by the Liturgical Movement in the twentieth century and which has found rather general acceptance in the Second Vatican Council.

Closely connected with the questions of by whom, where, and in what setting communion should be received was naturally the question of how often communion should be received. In general, from the time of the Middle Ages the frequency of the reception of communion by the general faithful had dropped drastically. This tendency in the Roman Catholic Church toward the infrequency of communion was in some ways only reinforced by the Protestant Reformation, Jansenism and certain aspects of the Enlightenment. In fact, one might very well expect German Enlightenment Catholics to play down the reception of the Eucharist in favor of the sermon. However, although, as has been shown above, the sermon did play a major role in the Aufklärung Catholic's ideal of worship service, the frequent reception of the Eucharist within the Mass was also emphasized by them. Thus, for example, already in the latter part of the eighteenth century Josef Lauber recommended that, with the exception of sinners, Christians ought to receive the Eucharist frequently.[206] A somewhat similar notion was expressed a generation later by Thomas Powondra, although he specifically suggested that the laity in general ought not receive the Eucharist more often than once a week; that, of course, would have been more than ten times as often as the rather frequently traditional four times a year.[207] About the same time, Hirscher also spoke of various means which would "make the reception of the sacrament again more frequent, which unfortunately and to the great disadvantage of Christian piety, had become ever more seldom."[208] As late as 1833 the rather moderate Aufklärung Catholic Franz Xaver Schmid wrote that, "The Church wishes that the faithful should receive the Holy Eucharist very often during the year."[209] Of course, those theologians quoted above who favored the general communion of all the faithful present at a Mass would also by that very fact be in favor of frequent communion, at least once a week, since all Catholics were obliged to attend Mass once a week.

There was also the kindred question of the age a person should receive his or her first communion. Not at all suprisingly already the latter part of the eighteenth century we find Catholic theologians writing that no particular age for the first communion of children could be set but rather that they must be mature enough, they must have attained the use of reason; such a decision ought not be automatically settled ahead of time in mechanical fashion.[210] Franz Xaver Schmid, writing later in the nineteenth century, did, however, specify the ages ten to twelve years as being the customary time of First Communion.[211]

Although, no doubt, the results of this emphasis on the reception of the Eucharist during the Mass by the laity had mixed results, depending, of course, on a variety of things, including the traditions of the area, but most of all on the ability and enthusiasm of the parish priest; there is at least some evidence that, contrary to the assertions of conservative Catholic Church historians,[212] large numbers of laity did receive communion during the Mass in "aufgeklärte" parishes. For instance, the then widely known liturgist and theologian, Vitus Anton Winter, reported: "Indeed in my parish often three, four to five thousand" receive communion, especially on feast days.[213] Indeed, it is difficult to imagine how the efforts of Wessenberg, Hirscher and the other Aufklärung Catholics quoted above in this regard could have had any effect other than to increase the reception of communion by the laity at Mass.

There was still one further aspect of the Eucharist which came under the urging of reform by a number of Aufklärung Catholics, namely, the reception of communion under both forms, bread and wine. In their returning to the biblical sources and in their emphasis on community, Aufklärung Catholics quite naturally tended to take a utraquist position. This position was held by Catholics as diverse as Werkmeister, who in the beginning of the nineteenth century advocated the reception of communion under both forms by the laity,[214] and Johannes Anton Theiner, who in 1830 advocated a similar position,[215] (both of whom were very critical of the Roman Catholic Church and both of whom have subsequently been excoriated by Roman Catholic Church historians), to famous and more or less well received Catholic theologians like Johann Baptist von Hirscher and Johann Adam Möhler. Hirscher, who in almost every instance seems to have in his early book on the Mass come out on the same side as the twentieth century Liturgical Movement and Vatican II, vigorously advocated wherever possible that the laity receive communion under both forms so that the essence of the Eucharist could thereby receive a better expression.[216] Even in his later and more conservative years, Hirscher still recommended utraquism and suggested that if the chalice were pressingly requested by the laity that it would be given.[217] But perhaps the most "respectable" of the Catholic theologians who spoke in favor of giving the chalice to the laity was Johann Adam Möhler. In his younger, more liberal years, Möhler very vigorously recommended the giving of the chalice to the laity, or at least making it available to them if they wished it.[218] He pointed out that this was the custom in the Church for the first twelve hundred years[219] and argued that this practice better expressed the essence of the Eucharist than the subsequent one in the Western Church.[220] Even in his more conservative period when he wrote his magnum opus *Symbolism* he still insisted: "Likewise, we would be very happy if it were left to the judgment of each individual as to whether or not he wished to drink from the sacred chalice."[221]

14. Church Music

The concerns of Aufklärung Catholics for reform in the liturgy, namely, the stress on the need for understanding on the part of all the people, the stress on the importance of developing a sense of community, the stress on moral instruction and motivation, and the stress on tolerance and what has since become known as ecumenism, also all had their effects on church music in that period. Thus, as has already been seen, there was in the latter part of the eighteenth century and the first part of the nineteenth century a strong development of vernacular church hymns, evidence for which are the many German hymn books that were published during this period.[222] In this same vein is a court decree from February 12, 1806: "In order to see that the music in the churches does not lead more to distraction and conversation than to the fostering of devotion one must look to it . . . also that such compositions are not produced which are composed more for a theater than the church."[223] In his monumental three-volume work on the history of the German church hymn Wilhelm Baümker stated that before the time of the Aufklärung, "all religious hymns possess more the character of subjective feeling and devotion than that of communal edification."[224] Aufklärung Catholicism, of course, worked in opposition to this tendency and, according to Baümker, rendered the indisputable service of "promoting the spread and expanded significance among the people of the church hymns (Kirchenlieder)."[225] Another church music historian, Rupert Giessler, rendered a similar verdict when he declared that the Aufklärung "was not solely a period of decline, as is evidenced in the history of the church hymn; rather it also bore within itself valuable and fruitful seeds of a new development."[226]

The emphasis in Aufklärung church music on moral instruction and motivation for the most part produced music and hymns that were "free from fanaticism and exaggeration in both thought and expression."[227] The titles themselves of many of the hymns indicate this characteristic. They included such as the following: On an Understanding Reading of the Bible, On the Love for Virtue, On the Growth in Virtue, On the Knowledge of Oneself, On the Overcoming of Faults in Charity, On Friendship, On Mercy, On the Avoidance of Pious Pride, and On the Enjoyment of Life. This particular ethical stress, which by no means was the only element present in Aufklärung church hymns, was perhaps well summed up in the words of a hymn by Christian Felix Weisse:

> What does it help me to be Christian,
> If I do not live like a Christian."

Or, in the lines of the hymn written by Christian Fürchtegott Gellert:

> For whoever knows your Holy Will
> And still does not do it with vigor;
> He is more reprehensible than the pagan
> And will be doubly punished."[228]

In their publishing of new church hymnals Aufklärung Catholics did not hesitate to include many Protestant hymns.[229] While the Aufklärung Catholics obviously thought that they were improving the religious quality of the Catholic worship service by drawing upon these Protestant hymns, conservative Catholic writers since that time have very often treated such action in itself as very close to treason. However, in speaking of this matter, the open, but cautious, Waldemar Trap wrote: "Nevertheless both prayer books [which included a large number of hymns by Protestant authors] almost throughout also contained many valuable and beautiful hymns."[230] One Aufklärung Catholic who did as much as, if not more than, anyone else in this area was Werkmeister. After Werkmeister became one of the court chaplains at Stuttgart he was asked by the Duke to produce a hymn book which would be usable by both Catholics and Protestants at the various court worship services. Werkmeister thereupon chose forty-eight hymns from various Protestant hymn books and the melodies from the Protestant Württemberg Melody Book so that the Protestants present at the Court could thereby support the singing of the Catholics (who apparently at this time were not used to congregational singing) in the Catholic Court Chapel.[231] In the introduction to this hymn book Werkmeister wrote: "In this collection only such hymns have been chosen which recommend practical Christianity and which can be sung by all Christians of our country without their being disturbed in their devotion by the presentation of a foreign belief."[232]

15. Church Architecture

These ideas of Aufklärung Catholics which emphasized the instruction and motivation of the people through the sermon and also the focusing of the congregation in a communal manner on the unitive sacrament of the Eucharist also had its ramifications for church architecture. Consequently, Aufklärung Catholics also spoke about the need of churches which would provide the proper sort of liturgical space to carry out their other ideas.[233] This meant, among other things, that when new churches were being built that they should not be too large, otherwise the effective unity of the congregation would be destroyed.[234] According to Aufklärung Catholic thought, all attention ought to be focused on the altar at which the Eucharist, including the sermon, was to be celebrated. Everything else was to be of secondary importance, or even better, to point to that central focus. Hence, Aufklärung Catholics made their own the recommendation of many Christian reformers throughout the centuries [235] that the early Christian custom of having only one altar in a church be reestablished.[236] To put this notion into action, on January 7, 1785, the Austrian government issued an order that in all newly built churches only one altar was to be set up.[237] And in those cases where the churches were already built and there were a number of altars in them the suggestion was made by at least one theologian that one altar be picked out and set up nearer the congregation, and on this altar the liturgy should be celebrated.[238] Of course this one altar upon which the Eucharist was to be celebrated was naturally to be so constructed that the priest would face the people.[239] Likewise, Aufklärung Catholics felt that this single altar should be a free standing altar set very near to, and wherever possible, in the midst of the people.[240] The altar was to be a low table-like altar[241] and was to have very little on it,[242] usually just a cross and four candles.[243] All of these recommendations of course sound very much like, not only the early church, but also the ideals promoted by the Liturgical Movement in the twentieth century and to a large extent enacted as a result of Vatican II.[244]

16. Missal and Mass Reforms

The Aufklärung Catholic concern for instruction, and particularly instruction that was biblically based, in the liturgy led several writers to wrestle with the problem of improving the missal. Here, however, as Waldemar Trapp noted, Aufklärung Catholics did not, for the most part, pass beyond theoretical suggestions. "Practical implementation was seldom and resulted really in only a few Mass formularies. A thoroughly worked out, reformed missal did not appear. The reasons for this were partly because of the hesitation even the extremists had about changing the Mass, and also the difficulty and magnitude of the undertaking."[245] Two of those who did produce new Mass formularies were Vitus Anton Winter, whose First German Critical Missal came out in 1810,[246] and Johann Baptist von Hirscher who in his dissertation, published in 1821,[247] included two self-composed Mass formularies.[248] One of the formularies was heavily dependent upon the current Latin Roman formulary, while the other was a considerably freer production. He offered these two formularies as possible patterns which contained everything which ought to be present in every Mass, although he also made allowances for the need of variations and coordination with the liturgical year.[249]

Beyond the question of the formulary for the Mass prayers which remained more or less essentially the same throughout the year was that of the readings at the Mass, which normally changed every day. Here a number of Aufklärung Catholics leveled some very severe criticisms at the current choice of readings. They felt that even when the readings were in the vernacular they still were not instructive enough because many of the texts chosen were not understandable. The choice of readings from the Epistles and the Gospels did not indicate any inter-connectedness and consequently were oftentimes impossible to understand and illogical.[250] Werkmeister, for instance, bitterly complained: "How was it possible to choose so many pieces in which nothing more than miracles were related, while at the same time the most instructive words of Jesus . . . which for ethical remarks offer the most fruitful material, remained unnoticed?"[251] Consequently, some theologians suggested that a new arrangement of readings be set up which would follow an historical order[252] in which the Epistles and Gospels chosenswould fit together as far as their content was concerned.[253] Others would have the new selection of readings be ordered more along the line of ethical ideas.[254] As a result of the wave of Catholic reaction in the 1840's and the blackening of the reputations and ideas of Aufklärung Catholics in the latter half of the nineteenth century and in the twentieth century this particular concern of the Aufklärung Catholics had to wait until Vatican II and its aftermath to find any thoroughgoing applications. In the years after Vatican II a whole series of rather broad changes in the Mass formulary and also the order of readings has taken place, much as many of the Aufklärung Catholics wished.

One other element of concern for the reform of the Mass by Aufklärung Catholics ought to be recorded here. That is, their serious criticism of the Masses said for the dead, which, many of them felt, tended to lead to a sense of irresponsibility among the common faithful. Such criticisms ranged in time from near the beginning of our period, 1804, to near its end, 1849. In the first instance Anton Winter wrote: "What could be easier than to give to the priest what one cannot in any case take along and thereby have oneself prayed out of purgatorial fire."[255] Johann Baptist von Hirscher, several decades after his early liberal work criticizing the liturgy of the Mass, poured forth a searing criticism of the trafficking in Masses for the dead and the corrupting effects it had on both the faithful and many of the priests:

"Besides the death-bed sacraments, what even more generally betrays the people into a false consolation as to the state of the departed, is the whole business of Masses for the dead. Whatever may yet be pressing upon the departed soul, may in the opinion of the common people be entirely removed by these sacrifices. If not, what are they for? They must, these poor folk argue, be of some advantage to the dead; and of course they buy off a portion of those sins which they committed in their lifetime and left undischarged. How happy then is the man who only dies rich, and who can buy any number of Masses, or found them in perpetuity! Riches are thus made an eternal possession, and the advantages of the *millionaire*, over the unhappy pauper, extend through all eternity! That these things are a gross mistake and a practical mischief, nobody can deny. And yet the clergy find these Masses such a vast profit to their purse!! I'm not complaining of prayers for the departed; at any rate, of *the invoking in their behalf of the sacrifice of Christ:* but one must be allowed to express his indignation, when he sees the people losing sight of the earnest work of life, and abandoning themselves to a false security; and when he knows that they are encouraged in these fatal delusions by the personal interests of their pastors."[256]

Very closely connected with the sentiments expressed here was the wish put forth by at least some Aufklärung Catholic writers to eliminate the paying of stipends for the administration of sacraments and for the celebration of Masses in general;[257] here again is another example of an Aufklärung Catholic goal finding its fulfillment only in the post-Vatican II era. Although such stipends have by no means been entirely eliminated in the years after the end of Vatican II, they are in practice falling away in an ever growing number of places.

17. *Sacramental Reforms:* A. *Baptism*

The Aufklärung Catholic liturgical reform goals of promoting the sense of community and the actuality of participation on the part of the faithful in the liturgy extended beyond the central act of worship, the Mass, to the sacraments as well. The sacraments of Baptism, Penance and Confirmation were the ones most obviously thereby affected. One of the things of course that many Aufklärung Catholics did was to use the various new German translations of the Ritual, which contained the prayers and rubrics for the administration of the sacraments. They felt that the use of the vernacular in the administration of the sacraments not only vastly enhanced the instructional aspect of the sacraments, but also contributed to the forging of a deeper sense of community, since the people would be bound together by understanding rather than ignorance. Some theologians urged that the sacrament of Baptism be administered in a festive, communal setting. Werkmeister, for example, urged that the entire congregation participate in the Baptisms every Sunday afternoon just before the afternoon devotions: "In order to make the rite of Baptism generally more festive and likewise edifying for the entire community, it would be good if the children who were born during the week would be baptized on the following Sunday."[258] There were also serious criticisms of the shrinking of the symbolic action in the rite of Baptism to the point where it had become meaningless: "For fifteen hundred years the baptized person put on a white garment . . . now the priest says, receive this white garment, but he hands the baptized person at the same time either nothing or merely lays a small white cloth on his head."[259]

B. *Penance*

One normally thinks of the sacrament of Penance, or Confession, in the Roman Catholic tradition as being something strictly private, conducted between the individual penitent and the priest in secrecy. However, many Aufklärung Catholics did not see this as necessarily entirely so. Many of them referred to the earlier practices of Christianity whereby penance and absolution was treated in a public, communal manner. They argued that at least the preparation for confession and the confession of guilt ought to be done publicly and communally.[260] In some instances this emphasis on the public and communal character of the sacrament of Penance did not include the giving of public and general absolution by the priest or the elimination of private confession; such a moderate position can be found in Hirscher[261] and Huber,[262] for example. Some, however, advocated a use of both general confession and private confession: "This brought me to the thought of establishing two kinds of confession, namely, private confession for those who believe themselves to be burdened with a mortal sin, and a general confession for those who were conscious only of the daily weaknesses and venial sins. The former visited me in my study, and here I had the opportunity to seach out the total condition of their soul. . . . Those in the second group appeared at twilight in the Church." There a common examination of conscience and fostering of contrition was undertaken, followed by absolution by the priest.[263] Still others felt that, "the general confession as a communal devotion is more deeply touching and it is therefore, as a preparation for Holy Communion seen as a communal meal, more effective."[264] Some of the more extreme Aufklärung Catholics argued that private confession was not of divine origin, as did Blau: "The reader will himself now draw the conclusion that private confession cannot be proved to be of divine law either from the Holy Scripture or from church tradition."[265]On the other hand, many Aufklärung Catholics spoke very highly of the sacrament of Penance, but were deeply disturbed over the manner in which it was administered.[266]

Hence, in general, the picture that emerges is one very much like the post-Vatican II scene. There was a general insistence on penance being a central element in Christianity and also that this expression of penance ought to be done more communally than traditionally was the case in recent times in Catholicism. Some went beyond this position to seriously criticize or reject the notion that private confession was of divine origin, but many, perhaps most, did not move in this direction. Nevertheless, the greater emphasis on public, general confession led to a lessening of the use of private confession. For Aufklärung Catholics, and like-minded Catholics of the post-Vatican II period, this could mean an improvement in the sense that it would tend to emphasize the importance of inner moral change in the individual and the community. For the traditional Catholic who felt that every reception of a sacrament was a gain, such a situation would probably have been viewed as a loss.

It would perhaps be of value to note in some detail a typical reaction of a conservative Catholic periodical to even the slightest move in the direction of stressing the communal aspect of the sacrament of Penance. In Bishop Keller's worship service ordinance for the diocese of Rottenburg in 1837 there was a section which covered the sacrament of Penance. In part it stated: "In connection with the preparation for worthily receiving the Holy Sacrament of the altar . . . no one with the consciousness of a grave sin should come forward to that Holy Sacrament without previous sacamental confession. A common preparation for this would seem to be particularly helpful and should include:

1.   Guidance to an earnest examination of the moral situation of the life and attitude of the penitent;
2.   A powerful stimulus to arouse a contrite attitude and a firm decision of amendment so that the penitent will be open to the absolution;

3. A general public confession of sins with additional prayers to forsake these sins. . . . This common devotion can, however, according to the prescriptions of the Catholic Church, in no case be seen as a sufficient preparation for the reception of the Holy Eucharist, as it is in itself according to basic Catholic principles absolutely self-understood that a confession of sins in general does not take the place of private confession and that the obligation of a special confession of sins before a priest cannot be suspended."

The commentary in *Der Katholik* on this brief section of Bishop Keller's worship service ordinance ran for some eight pages of fine print. The commentary in general was quite acid, accusing the ordinance of "easily leading to Protestant attitudes," among other things. Despite the disclaimers of eliminating or downgrading private confession explicitly stated in the ordinance, the *Katholik* commentator had the following to say: "Because the episcopal prescription itself, despite all its clauses, reservations and inhibitions, could be merely a sought for means by some lukewarm and heterodox priests to, if not entirely eliminate private confession out of hand, nevertheless so stifle it that it would become ineffective, and this under a legal form, it is to be feared, as is said to be the case in Württenberg and Baden, that one will be satisfied with a general confession of sins, and that without further admonition . . . without further question or probing of the condition of the conscience absolution will be given. . . . Finally, it is contrary to the spirit of the Catholic Church to wish to water down everything with words . . . and to substitute such a blather and jargon [*Wortemacherei und Phrasengeklingel*]."[267]

C. Confirmation

The sacrament of Confirmation has never had a really major role to play in the liturgical life of the Catholic. Following in this tradition Confirmation also did not figure greatly in the reform concerns of Aufklärung Catholics. Nevertheless, many of them did urge that Confirmation ought to be more adequately prepared for and administered in a more worthy and festive manner.[268] However, one point that Aufklärung Catholics did promote which finds an echo in the post-Vatican II period is that the administration of Confirmation should not be limited to the bishop. This was recommended because in many places there was a dearth of bishops or, at any rate, a dearth of effective bishops, which meant that for very extended periods of time, many years and even decades, Confirmation would not be administered in many areas. Hence it was recommended that to avoid the evil consequences of this situation the pastors be allowed to administer Confirmation.[269] In arguing for a return to such a practice Friderich Brenner argued: "For six hundred years both choir bishops and priests administered Confirmation in certain cases. At present the bishop alone administers Confirmation; the right to do this is taken from the priests so that only with a special papal dispensation, and indeed extremely seldom, are they allowed to exercise this right."[270]

18. Reform of the Ritual

The book which contains the prayers and rubrics for the administration of the various sacraments and also various blessings and sacramentals is the Ritual. Before the latter part of the nineteenth century it was quite customary for each diocese to either recommend the use of one of several versions of the Ritual then in existence, or to produce one of its own. Particularly in the latter part of the eighteenth century and the beginning of the nineteenth century these Rituals more and more began to appear in the vernacular languages, the reasons being the usual pastoral ones typical of the Aufklärung. Two early moderate versions of the Ritual were published in 1809 and 1812 by Karl Schwarzel[271] and Herenäus Haid.[272] There was very little change in these Rituals from the earlier Latin formularies, except the occasional substitution of a German translation of the Latin, and in Schwarzel's Ritual even then the Latin text was usually included in a parallel column. However, somewhat earlier, in 1803, another moderate version of the Ritual was published by Ludwig Busch,[273] moderate in the sense that it stayed extremely close to the traditional Latin formulary of the Ritual, but it was translated entirely into German, and was consequently well received by Aufklärung Catholics.[274] Then in 1806 Beda Pracher published a German version of the Ritual[275] and in 1811 Werkmeister produced another German Ritual, largely compiled out of the work of others.[276] Still another Ritual was published by Anton Selmar.[277] More important, perhaps, than many, if not all, of these earlier German versions of the Ritual was the one produced by Vitus Anton Winter in 1813.[278] Winter's Ritual received its importance partly because it was particularly effectively done and partly because of Winter's reputation and influential positions in both the ecclesiastical and academic worlds.[279] One further indication of its importance was the fact that in 1830 it was reworked and put out in a new edition by Jakob Brand, the bishop of Limburg.[280] In addition to these, and other, editions of partially or totally German versions of the Ritual in the early part of the nineteenth century, a large number of improved German formularies for various parts of the Ritual appeared in numerous newspapers and journals.[281]

Nothing further of any special significance occured in this area until 1831, when Wessenberg finally, after great hesitation, some four years after he was out of his ecclesiastical office, published his German version of the Ritual.[282] Like other Aufklärung Catholics, Wessenberg was deeply concerned about the active participation of the laity in the liturgy; this concern was very much reflected in the prayers, rules and structure of his Ritual. Even the title of his Ritual includes the words: "At the same time a book of edification for the faithful." Of course, the instruction aspect of the liturgy played a large role in the form and content of Wessenberg's Ritual, but certainly not an exclusive role. In the various prayers and blessings emphasis was put upon seeking not material but rather spiritual goods. Wesssenberg underlined this point when he insisted that the instructions, prayers, hymns and ceremonies contained in the Ritual had as their goal "to lift the spirit and the heart of those present to God and to make an advantageous and effective impression on their feelings which would lead to the improvement and sanctification of their lives."[283] And to accomplish all this Wessenberg insisted that the proper handling of the role of the priest was essential: "What the liturgical leader can never impress too deeply on his soul is this: the effect of liturgical ceremonies, forms and words is very much limited by the dignity, vitality and propriety of the personal conduct of the liturgical leader. . . . The holy must be handled in a holy manner! Then it will also arouse holy sentiments."[284]

Wessenberg's new Ritual had a very enthusiastic reception among a large number of the clergy, particularly in southwestern Germany. Even the ultra-conservative Catholic historian Adolf Rösch noted that the chapters of Sigmaringen and Veringen, as soon as they heard that Wessenberg's Ritual was about to be published, unanimously subscribed to receive the first edition, which they did on January 25, 1831.[285] For decades the judgment on Wessenberg's Ritual pretty well depended on the polemic lining up of liberal versus conservative. However, in 1939 the quite objective Waldemar Trapp spoke of the prayers therein as being: "worked out with particular love. . . . In general the Ritual contained many things of great beauty and value. . . . Wessenberg's Ritual is one of the richest of the Aufklärung."[286]

Perhaps the most dramatic evidence of the popularity of Wessenberg's Ritual, in southwestern Germany at least, came in 1835 when Archbishop Boll of Freiburg published a new Ritual for his diocese.[287] Adolf Rösch tells the story as succinctly as possible: "The contents [of the 1835 Freiburg Ritual] is dogmatically correct; nevertheless the editor believed it necessary to accomodate the current attitude among the clergy and the people by employing the mother tongue in the widest possible fashion, by a special emphasis on the edifying aspect (many portions of the Wessenberg Ritual were taken over either word for word or with only a very small change, so as to accomplish this) and by the leaving out of a host of blessings and exorcisms. Nevertheless an angry storm broke out against this Ritual."[288] "It still required a great effort to bring the priests into submission."[289] In many places the clergy petitioned for the right to continue to use the Wessenberg Ritual along with the newly published Freiburg Ritual.[290] A Pastor Sprissler from Empfingen was even more defiant, when he wrote to the chancery office: "Moreover it [the new Freiburg Ritual] has not arisen in legal fashion and it suffers criminally in several places; namely, the *exorcism in Baptism is contrary to Catholic doctrine*, as I beg to point out, and it appears therefore as a misuse of the mystical power of the Church. The speaking of the formulas of the sacraments in Latin I hold to be both laughable and unbiblical. The threatened suspension, which, unheard of in this diocese, has aroused so much astonishment and resistance, does not burden me because it is obviously illegal and powerless until a Ritual is adopted in legal manner through the decision of a Synod."[291] However, the Freiburg Chancery was adamant and, with the growing support of the civil governments, it was able to force the

acceptance of the new Ritual. Here again can be seen the strength of
Aufklärung Catholicism, particularly among the clergy in southwestern
Germany, and the willingness to follow authority, namely Wessenberg's
authority, who had been the administrator of that area for some twenty-five
years, but at the same time a willingness to resist another authority which,
though formally correct, appeared to them to be usurping in spirit the real
Christian authority. Again, as in many areas of church life, the authoritarian
forces from above began to triumph more and more consistently from the
latter part of the 1830's onward.

19. Extensive Breviary Reforms

Another important portion of the Catholic liturgy which came in for
strong criticism and cries for reform by Aufklärung Catholics was that of the
breviary. The criticisms were wide ranging, including, for example, the
tendency of the breviary to promote a mechanical sort of prayer. The
moderate Hirscher wrote, "Concerning the composition of this book of
devotion there are now very many things which with the greatest rectitude can
be stated with certainty: The book itself in our times has outlived its
usefulness; it has on this account long since promoted mere lip prayers and
mechanical recitation."[292] Another area of serious criticism of the breviary
was its cult of the saints, particularly the readings of the lives of the saints
found in the second nocturne of matins. One Aufklärung Catholic, for
example, spoke of the "breviary where truth and falsehood (lectionis secundi
nocturni) are mixed together."[293] Also in general Aufklärung Catholics
tended to think that the breviary was too long for diocesan priests, and badly
structured for their needs, although in some form it would make sense in the
monastic life, from which it sprang, although there too it obviously would
have to be reformed.[294] The very widespread antithetical attitude toward the
breviary is perhaps aptly expressed in a poem from that period: "The priest
who is a wise man and forgets his breviary before the need of his brothers is an
ornament of mankind. The priest who is a fool and feeds only on the breviary
from among the Church's storehouse is a depraved beast."[295]

The attitudes on what to do about the unsatisfactory condition of the
breviary were spread over a broad range. On one extreme it was
recommended that the breviary be done away with entirely as an obligatory
prayerbook for diocesan priests. Winter, for example, felt that since the
breviary developed only through custom and since it had lost its purpose as far
as the present was concerned, it should therefore be done away with by the
ecclesiastical authorities.[296] Werkmeister went even farther than Winter,
arguing that he "thought much too narrowly. Just as the breviary was
introduced through custom, so can it also be set aside through a contrary
custom."[297] Most Aufklärung Catholics however advocated not a total
abolition of the breviary but a varying range of significant changes in it.[298]

The move to reform the breviary began in many ways already in the latter part of the seventeenth century in France. A new breviary appeared in 1680 for the archdiocese of Paris, edited by the Archbishop Francois de Harlay, who wrote to his clergy concerning it, that his goal was to eliminate everything that was improper, that could give the appearance of superstition, that poorly reflected the dignity of the Church and early Christianity.[299] The influence of this breviary on most French breviaries for the next hundred years or so, and through them on the ones in Germany, was very large. In 1791 eighty different French dioceses had their own breviary, whose central characteristics were as follows: (1) The entire Psalter was to be prayed through entirely in a week, (2) the most important portions of the Old and New Testaments were to be read once each year, (3) the responses also were to be taken from Holy Scriptures, (4) the office was not to be too long and therefore a burden to the diocesan clergy, and (5) the breviary was most particularly to be purified of any suspicious saints' legends.[300] Already by 1780 the influence of these reforms in the French breviaries began to manifest itself in Germany. In that year a new edition of the breviary for the diocese of Cologne was published, and incorporated many of the French reforms. From this point forward many of the other German dioceses followed suit by putting out revised editions of the breviary.[301]

Despite the more or less effective reforms of the breviary in the latter part of the eighteenth century the question of the obligation of the diocesan priests to recite the breviary was raised already in 1789 in a document submitted by the archdiocesan chancery in Mainz.[302] This obligation was further questioned not only by Catholics such as Winter and Werkmeister, as mentioned above, but also by Johannes Theiner,[303] and two canonists, Michl and Brendel.[304]

Aufklärung Catholics however did not normally advocate the elimination of the obligation of saying the breviary for priests, or grant dispensation from that obligation, without substituting what they felt was a more worthwhile practice, namely, the regular reading of the Bible. In 1779 the pseudonymous Louis Garson called for the elimination of the obligation of the breviary and the substitution of the reading of the Holy Scriptures (with an additional quarter hour's meditation and prayer) within the next two years.[305] Even the very moderate Franz Andreas Schramm wrote in the year before the outbreak of the French Revolution that he recognized the obligation to recite the breviary, on the part of priests, but: "I do not however wish to say whether it would not be better if one were to eliminate certain legends of the saints from the breviary and in their place substitute the Divine Scriptures."[306] In the following year (1789) however, the recommendation of the archdiocesan chancery in Mainz, mentioned in the previous paragraph, stated not only that parish priests ought not to be obliged to recite the breviary, but rather, should be obliged to read the Holy Scriptures and perform other spiritual exercises according to time and opportunity.[307] The same idea was continued into the nineteenth century by Vitus Anton Winter who argued that only the reading of the Sacred Scriptures should be made obligatory for priests.[308] This notion of substituting the reading of the Bible for the recitation of the breviary clearly caught on in many places in Germany, as is indicated at least for the southwestern portion of Germany by the statement made in 1817 by Wessenberg to Cardinal Consalvi, the Vatican Secretary of State: "Dispensations from the obligation of the breviary were never given without putting in its place other works of devotion or meditation on the Holy Scriptures. In recent years they became infrequent and always only granted for pressing reasons."[309] The custom obviously continued to have great popularity through at least the first third of the nineteenth century, for in 1832, five years after the removal of Wessenberg as administrator of the diocese of Constance, the Freiburg chancery responded to an inquiry by a group of diocesan priests concerning the obligation of saying the breviary in a manner that indicated the reading of the Scriptures and the Church Fathers was of greater importance than reading the breviary: "Concerning the inquiry and the proposal about the praying of the breviary by priests it is self-understood that the professional activities and preparations, especially meditation, reading of the Holy Scriptures and the Fathers, take precedence over the reading of the breviary; however, such omission because of sloth cannot be excused. . . . We do not wish to limit any priest nor burden his conscience: if in his private devotions he would choose those parts of the breviary which speak most to him and add to them the above mentioned reading of the Scriptures and the Fathers, or even another edifying book."[310]

One of those books of devotion that was very popular as a substitute for the breviary, among other things, was the four volume "German Breviary" by Johannes Thaddäus Antonius Dereser[312] published in 1792. The structure of this four volume work was in a number of ways not unlike some breviaries used by religious orders in contemporary Catholicism. It was divided into four main parts: morning prayers and readings, prayers and readings before and after Mass, afternoon prayers and readings, and evening prayers and readings. As was traditional, many psalms were used, but only those "which are particularly instructive and edifying for Christians."[313] Great stress was placed on the reading of the New Testament (arrangements were made so that it was read entirely in the course of one year) and commentary on the readings. Readings of the saints' lives were reduced to either brief portions of those saints about which something was written in the Scriptures or a reading concerning the general catagory of the saint in question, e.g., martyrs, confessors, etc. "The pious recollection of the other saints is left to the decision of the one praying."[314] This German language breviary "found general applause in Germany. It has been expressly recommended by the episcopal authorities in several dioceses, e.g., Cologne, Augsburg, Worms, and Constance. It is greatly in use in the bishoprics of Osnabrück, Münster, Cologne, Speyer, Constance, and so forth."[315] Its great popularity is also attested to by the fact that between 1792 and 1847 some sixteen editions of it appeared.[316] Although according to its title it was specifically designed for nuns and "every good Christian," it quickly found wide use among the clergy as a substitute, or partial substitute, for the recitation of the Latin breviary. In 1804 the organ of Wessenberg's pastoral conferences carried a favorable review of the forthcoming 1805 edition of Dereser's breviary and suggested that it would be better if priests were free to choose books like that of Dereser's rather than the Roman breviary.[317] Another small indication of how the use of Dereser's German Breviary by the clergy caught on is a question given in the clergy exam of 1809 in the kingdom of Württemberg which stated that a young priest confessed that he found that he had not sufficient time to read the breviary and consequently substituted the daily reading of the German Breviary by Dereser and spent some additional time meditating on the reading from the Old and New Testament found therein; moreover he held that this practice was better than the recitation of the breviary. "What decision should be made concerning this problem?"[318] As a matter of fact this question was answered by "the certainly authentic Catholic prince-bishop of Würzburg, Franz Ludwig, who not only uses the German Breviary for his own edification, but also allows his younger priests to pray it rather than the Latin breviary. . . ."[319] Wessenberg, as noted above, of course often granted the same permission.[320]

While in the first half of the nineteenth century the reading of the Scriptures and books like Dereser's German Breviary grew rapidly in popularity, among clergy and laity, the reading of the Latin breviary by priests seemed to drop off proportionately. On December 18, 1801, for example, Herder in Meersburg wrote to Wessenberg: "The breviary in its present condition finds approval by extremely few priests who attempt to pray regularly. Some do not recite it at all. Therefore an improvement appears necessary."[321] A decade later one author wrote that, "in the present time it appears to me that the number of those who do not pray the breviary is far greater than the number of those who do."[322] Some years later, in 1821, Werkmeister again declared that it is not true that most priests in Germany still pray the breviary daily.[323] That this tendency for priests not to recite the Latin breviary expanded in the next dozen or so years is attested to by the 1832 document from the Freiburg chancery office, referred to above, which stated that it did not wish to bind all priests to the recitation of the breviary.[324] The conclusion from this and other evidence drawn by the conservative Catholic Church historian Adolf Rösch is that, "the general conviction that in the period of the Aufklärung in question, 1800–1850, the praying of the breviary also generally fell into complete disuse among the Hohenzollern clergy [southwestern Germany] finds in the foregoing facts strong supporting evidence."[325]

Thus it seems fairly clear that large numbers of priests in Germany, particularly in southwestern Germany but also in the Rhineland and Silesia and elsewhere, not only severly criticized the structure of the Roman breviary, but more and more began to substitute the reading of the Scriptures and books such as Dereser's German Breviary for it—a situation quite similar to that of the 1970's in most of Catholicism.

20. *Battle Against Superstitions*

While almost all of the matters discussed up to this point in regard to the liturgical reform of Aufklärung Catholicism could be thought of as being essentially positive in thrust, Aufklärung Catholics did specifically and vigorously oppose a number of things which they thought of as abuses. They were, for example, quite concerned with the elimination of what they termed superstitions among the masses of the people. It should be recalled that it was only with the Aufklärung that the hunting down and killing of old women as witches was finally stamped out as an acceptable practice in Western civilization. In fact, in the official new edition of the Ritual of the diocese of Augsburg published in 1764 there can be found blessings against bewitching, a blessing for a perfume against bewitching, and also one for bewitched animals.[326] In a work on moral theology published in 1785[327] the author referred to a whole series of superstitions that were widespread among the people at that time in connection with practically all Christian religious activities, including even various sacraments. For instance, it was thought that a new mother was not allowed to leave her room or hear Mass until after she had undergone the churching ceremony.[328] Confirmation was thought to be an effective means against sleepwalking or nightmares.[329] Likewise "many believe it is forbidden to work on days during which one was at the table of the Lord."[330] There, of course, was a wealth of good luck pieces, charms, etc. that were supposedly connected with the essence of Christianity, as for example, the then very famous Saint Luke's card (*Lukaszettel*).[331]

In many ways of course it was not easy for Aufklärung Catholics to attack the various superstitious practices, since they were held by many to be a valid part of Christianity. (If this seems difficult for a contemporary Catholic to grasp, let him recall the almost universally accepted customs of going in and out of a church on All Soul's Day in order to say the few brief prayers to attain a large number of *totius quotius* indulgences for the dead, or the wearing of numerous scapulars and miraculous medals, etc., that are beginning to fade into disuse only after Vatican II. Many Catholic theologians after the Second Vatican Council would consider such things as quite close to superstitions, whereas more conservative theologians would cry out volubly that they were attacking Christian doctrine thereby.) Nevertheless, Aufklärung Catholics did make headway against superstition among the people, as evidenced by the statement published already in 1791: "The Aufklärung in Dillingen has already spread so far that I could give a lecture on the ineffectiveness of magic without running the danger of bringing my orthodoxy into suspicion. [He then significantly added] Nevertheless this lecture did cause a ferment."[332] Thus, the battle against superstition in Catholicism was vigorously engaged by Aufklärung Catholics as long as they had strength, that is, into the 1830's and 40's.

21. *Pilgrimages and Processions*

One of the practices Aufklärung Catholics vigorously opposed was the excess of pilgrimages. This might seem surpising to twentieth century Catholics, particularly of North America, since even before Vatican II pilgrimages did not appear to play a very significant role in the life of modern Catholics. However, it must be recalled that during the Middle Ages and into the nineteenth century processions and pilgrimages figured very importantly in the life of Catholics.

The reasons for Aufklärung Catholics' opposition to most processions and pilgrimages were varied. It was felt that they often led to the encouragement of a superstitious attitude, as if, for example, God could only, or more effectively, be praised and petitioned in one place rather than in another; that they were too often the occasions for encouraging slothfulness, the leading of a dissolute life by overeating and overdrinking and sexual immorality, particularly on those pilgrimages which were overnight affairs; that they led to the serious degradation of the parish worship and religious instruction.

Waldemar Trapp noted that the,"battle against the excess of pilgrimages was almost general. The state and bishops opposed them, and even the pastors spoke of them critically."[333] Not only did the more extreme Aufklärung Catholics oppose the pilgrimages,[334] but also the more moderate Aufklärung Catholics.[335] A number of bishops published pastoral letters or other decrees which severely criticized the current practice of pilgrimages, as for example Bishop Klemens Wenzeslaus of Augsburg,[336] Friedrich von Erthal, bishop of Mainz[337] and the bishop of Seggau,[338] and later in the 1820's the Archbishop of Cologne, Baron Spiegel.[339] In fact, "time and again one finds in the decrees of the bishops of that time directives that the essentials must be emphasized more vigorously, as well as the battle against abuses."[340]

Wessenberg, of course, also took part in the battle against the excesses of processions and pilgrimages at that time. On March 4, 1809, he issued a somewhat lengthy ordinance concerning pilgrimages.[341] These regulations included the forbidding of religous festivities at pilgrimage spots unless there was a pilgrimage priest appointed to conduct them, the forbidding of the sale of various pilgrimage booklets and hymns, or the leaving of votives and other indications of answered prayers (crutches, etc.) in the pilgrimage chapels. There was, of course, a certain amount of resistance to these ordinances, particularly on the part of the people, but for the most part the clergy was very much in favor of the ordinances, that is, the diocesan clergy.[342] Of course, often certain priests of religious orders were displeased with the ordinances because they were thereby cut off from their livelihood. Still, these ordinances and the general impact of the efforts of Aufklärung Catholicism tended to reduce drastically the practice of pilgrimages, at least in southwestern Germany.[343] However, it should be noted that with the removal of

Wessenberg and the general decline of the influence of Aufklärung Catholicism that the practice of pilgrimages was at least to some extent reestablished in southwestern Germany, particularly after 1840.[344]

22. Fasting

Another ancient practice of the Christian Church which at least some Aufklärung Catholics opposed was that of fasting. The positions taken range from that of Frantisek Nahlovsky who in 1848 urged that the law of fasting be moderated,[345] and that of Wessenberg, and others, who granted permissions for breaking one's fast in the morning before receiving Holy Communion,[346] to that of Aloys Pflanz and Fridolin Huber, who were in favor of eliminating the law of fasting altogether.[347] Those who opposed the law of fasting did so because they felt it contributed little or nothing to a person's spiritual or ethical improvement and that it could lead to a sense of self-righteousness, morbidity, or a mechanical-superstitious attitude toward religious "practice." Huber once wrote: "Eat what is cheapest, most healthy and what is most wholesome for the spirit."[348] Another time he wrote that he loves no other kind of fasting than that of moderation.[349] (Although this question of fasting and abstinence was really a quite small point for Aufklärung Catholicism, and also for contemporary Catholicism, it is interesting to note that in the aftermath of Vatican II the Church authorities almost entirely eliminated the eucharistic fast and also the other laws of fast and abstinence throughout the year.)

23. Cult of Saints

One of the areas of the Catholic liturgy which since before the time of the Reformation has been the object of innumerable reform attempts is the cult of the saints. Aufklärung Catholics were very especially horrified at the excesses of the cult of the saints that had developed during the baroque period. As a consequence they spoke out vigorously against the various excesses of the veneration of saints.[350] One even finds bishops, as Klemens Wenzeslaus of Mainz, writing vigorously against the excesses of the veneration of the saints, for, he felt, this often led to giving greater honor to the dead saints than the living God.[351] The Aufklärung Catholic attitude was perhaps best summed up by Johann Baptist von Hirscher when he wrote that a great danger of the cult of the saints is that it could so easily turn into "worship service of the saints: for now *they* are believed in, *they* are loved, and in *them* is trust placed."[352]

One of the specific things that Aufklärung Catholics objected to as excesses of the cult of the saints was the domination by devotion to the saints in most of the Masses throughout the liturgical year. Winter wrote "that in the missal [devotion to the saints] takes unto itself almost every day of the year; even Sunday, the day of the Lord is not excluded."[353] Peuger argued that it was improper "to direct one's devotion to the saints . . . where that most honored treasure [the Eucharist] is publicly set before us for adoration."[354]

Even the rather cautious Sailer, in speaking of matters that needed reform, listed as one, "the too great stress on petitioning the saints that may have developed in the Masses in later times."[355]

Peuger, in the statement just cited, was by no means the only Aufklärung Catholic who objected to the excesses in parading the pictures and statues of saints. Bishop Klemens Wenzeslaus for one, specifically objected to the over-decorating of saint's pictures with gaudy colors and luxurious cloth.[356] And even the conservative Sebastian Brunner, writing in the middle of the nineteenth century, stated: "The carrying around of larger-than-life-size statues of the saints with clothing of linen, silk, and gold material . . . then the brotherhood feasts which, the more they moved away from the pious direction of their founder, the more they likewise went in for pure external ostentation, gave occasion for derision."[357] Perhaps one of the most interesting ecclesiastical rescripts on this matter of the pictures and statues of saints was that of the worship ordinance of Bishop Keller of Rottenburg, of 1837. There he spoke of the need to avoid having improper pictures and statues of the saints in churches, and recalled a previous ordinance of 1827 in which all clothed pictures or statues of saints were forbidden in the churches. It is an enlightening commentary on the customs of the time that at this point Bishop Keller felt compelled to recall a portion of the statement of the Council of Trent on the veneration of the saints: "Concerning the veneration of the pictures of the saints, likewise everything should be avoided which would be superstitious or indeed idolatrous; in particular, it may not be believed that a power dwells in the picture, on which account it is honored, or as if it were to be petitioned for something, or as if in any way a trust were to be placed in the image, as previously heathens did when they placed their hope in pictures and images."[358]

In much of Catholic tradition one of the most important things that saints were supposed to do was to intercede with God for favors to the petitioner. This notion came in for a variety of criticisms from Aufklärung Catholics. Many, like Hirscher, for example, granted the validity of the notion of the intercession of the saints, although he did not wish to stress it. Beda Pracher cut a bit closer to the edge of the old tradition; he granted that, "the wish that they would intercede with God for us can at least arouse in us a wholesome striving to make us worthy of their friendship."[359] Philipp Josef Brunner[360] wrote: "The calling on the saints, as the veneration of them, is not necessary, is not commended, but is only allowed. . . . It is not an article of faith that the saints hear and understand all the prayers which we direct to them. . . . It is not an article of faith that God always attends to the intercession of the saints. . . . It is not an article of faith that saints always have an insight into what would contribute to our true welfare. . . . It would be an unconscionable superstition if we were to accept the nonsense that God does not hear us if we petition directly to Him for something, if we come to Him without a patron who supports our petition through his intercession. . . . It would also be a despicable superstition if we imagined God to be like an earthly monarch and the saints like his courtiers to whom we must first turn if we wish to receive something from Him."[361] Brunner also noted that in the Patristic period, "it did not occur to any Christian to call upon a saint or to build churches and altars in their honor."[362] Werkmeister went the full way on the criticism of the intercession of the saints by insisting that the only value in the veneration of the saints was in the imitation of them; to call upon them for intercession he felt was superstitious.[363] But even before the question of intercession could arise Brunner pointed out that, "it is not an article of faith that this or that saint really is a saint. . . . Indeed, it is not even an article of faith that all these persons which one holds to be saints really lived,"[364] which, in light of the long list of saints that were eliminated from the official rolls by Rome in 1969, was a rather prophetic statement.[365]

Another important aspect of the cult of the saints that was severely criticized by Aufklärung Catholics was the number of feast days, mostly saints days, which had been over the years raised to Holy Days of Obligation, that is, days other than Sundays on which there was an obligation to hear Mass and avoid manual labor. Aufklärung Catholic theologians and churchmen objected to the overabundance of such days largely because they felt they overstressed the importance of the saints, and because they believed that many of these feast days were largely occasions for encouraging slothfulness and various elements of a dissipated life, because of the various fairs and festivities that were developed in connection with such holidays. The movement to reduce the number of Holy Days of Obligation was also at the same time supported by many people in business and government for reasons of economic development.

The first major reduction in the number of the Holy Days of Obligation in German lands came on June 22, 1771, through an edict of Pope Clement XIV (the same Pope who supressed the Jesuits), which was issued for all Austrian lands. This edict eliminated nineteen Holy Days of Obligation! Since part of the diocese of Constance was then Austrian territory, Bishop Max Christoph of Constance petitioned Pope Clement XIV on March 21, 1778, for an indult (permission) to extend the reduction of Holy Days of Obligation to the entire diocese of Constance. The request was granted. In addition to this large number of Holy Days of Obligation generally observed, it should also be noted that many individual parishes also observed a large number, even up to twenty, of additonal feast days on which there was no work and people attended church and various festivities.[366] There was of course a goodly amount of resistance to the elimination of these holidays throughout the rest of the eighteenth century. However early in the nineteenth century "Wessenberg worked energetically, and finally with complete success toward the total elimination of the downgraded Holy Days of Obligation."[367] He accomplished this largely, through his careful, pastoral conferences which he regularly held with his clergy.[368] Baron Spiegel, Archbishop of Cologne, also reduced the number of holidays in his jurisdiction in the 1820's.[369] (One of the deans of Wessenberg's diocese responded with a suggestion that finds an echo in contemporary Catholicism: Dean Weiger suggested that the feasts of the Apostles and the feast of Saint John the Baptist be celebrated on the following Sundays so as to avoid any undue sensationalism among the people.[370] In contemporary Catholicism surveys have been conducted among the faithful to see whether or not they would like the various Holy Days of Obligation maintained as they are, eliminated altogether, or transferred to the following Sunday.)

Lest it be thought that Aufklärung Catholicism was able to eliminate the abuses of the veneration of the saints everywhere in Germany and for all subsequent time, or that their protests were gross exaggerations, it would be helpful to recall what was written in 1849 by Johann Baptist von Hirscher, the moderate Catholic theologian, who for the most part has been accepted by even conservative Catholic theologians and Church historians. "Without entering further into the subjet of our deficiencies, I must yet touch upon one point more: I mean, the customary veneration of saints. Against the practice in itself, I have not only no prejudice, but in my *Erörterungen*, I have particularly, and I think on tenable grounds, defended it: still, even there I took occasion to remark, that it has its admixture of imperfections, and that it has assumed an improper and disproportioned importance, in relation to other parts of the public service. Nobody will be disposed to dispute this, who will only observe the numerical proportion between Masses *de ea*, and those *de Sanctis*. Would it not be sufficient merely to insert the name of the Saint, on whose day the celebration may fall, in the ordinary commemoration of Saints, as it occurs in every Mass? I have further said, that many of the faithful devote to some especial saint their particular veneration, and that they become so absorbed in the adoration of this saint, as to pay to their patron what is due to God alone, even the tribute of pious trust and ardent love. This is a notorious fact, and one of daily occurrence. I added, moreover, that the holidays, commemorating divers saints, were frequently made the occasion of a vast concourse of the populace, and of many gross immoralities. This is also notorious. Besides, these holidays are often celebrated with a degree of magnificence not customary on the highest festivals of Christ Himself: a fact which must lead to a deplorable confusion of ideas. I might have further said, that every country every place, every individual, every conceivable thing, must have its patron saint, and that we are fast approximating to the heathen notion of the government of the universe, with all its consequences. At all events, these are improprieties which, in the highest degree, demand the immediate attention of the Church."[371]

24. Marian Piety

An additional aspect of the cult of the saints that Aufklärung Catholics saw as needing reform was aptly expressed in a work written by Werkmeister at the beginning of the last century: *To the Immodest Venerators of the Saints, Especially of Mary*.[372] That there were exaggerations in Marian piety is borne out in the history of the past fifteen hundred years. Two tiny examples from the eighteenth century can be seen in one prayerbook where Mary was addressed as, "my only refuge," and, "All Powerful Empress, the Destroyer of the Powers of Hell and Ruler of all the World."[373] Werkmeister, Wessenberg, and many others, wished to retain Marian piety, but on a biblical base. As noted earlier, Wessenberg wrote, "The life of the Blessed Virgin Mary cannot always be preached upon because the Holy Scriptures do not give us a detailed account of the life of Mary, but rather only a few fragments."[374] On a similar basis Werkmeister wished to slowly eliminate all of the Marian feasts except that of the Annunciation, which of course is based on the Gospel of Saint Luke.[375]

The part of Marian piety that seemed to come in for the most stringent criticism was the Rosary. As mentioned before, Wessenberg forbade the recitation of the Rosary aloud during Mass, "because, as good as the individual parts of it are in themselves, it is not suited for devotion at Mass."[376] Here again the moderate Hirscher stated well the central position of many Aufklärung Catholics on the Rosary: "There should be caution as to putting into the hands of the people such formularies as tend to encourage lip-praying, or devotions which thought and reflection do not accompany. The saying over and over again, fifty times, of a short and particular form, as in the recitation of the Rosary, leads directly to this grave mistake. Those who undertake, now-a-days, to cry up so enthusiastically this exercise of the Rosary, appear to have little idea of the responsibility which they assume. Do they forget, that in favouring it, they are recommending a sort of prayer purely mechanical, which, unless thus encouraged, would not last as long as the formulary itself. Nobody can underrate the immense importance of the realities of religion which are involved in the exercise: but why then encourage the perpetual repetition of the mere letter, instead of presenting them one by one, accompanied by some substantial suggestion, and followed by a collect, or some appropriate canticle, adapted to inspire the sentiments and meditations which ought to be produced."[377]

Not all Catholic theologians were as mild in their criticism. Dorsch and Blau wrote, "We wish to see the Rosary completely banned, because it stretches a devotion out so impossibly long. The counting off of the beads is a mere mechanical action during which the heart certainly remains completely empty."[378] Peuger felt that it was an unnecessary, inappropriate, and purposeless prayer, too bad even for the masses, whose thoughtlessness it does everything to further.[379] Pracher referred to the Rosary as "the most miserable of all prayers,"[380] and went on to say that, "since every prayer which does not take place in the heart and the mouth is more sinful than fruitful, and since the Rosary, which is repetitious, can very easily become that pagan lip service of which Jesus spoke in Matthew 6, the efforts of the pastor to introduce fruitful prayers is praiseworthy and is to be greeted with gratitude."[381]

The last remark of Pracher's reflects a practice among Aufklärung Catholic priests: "There is no enlightened pastor who is not aware of the inappropriate and distorting character of this prayer and who does not at every opportune moment seek to substitute for it a better devotion more attuned to the present spirit of the times."[382] Dr. Herenäus Haid, for example, published a two volume work containing the Rosary in sixteen different versions, including his own contemporary suggestion.[383] This "remodeled" Rosary found great use, at least in the diocese of Constance, and was also further remodeled by each individual pastor.[384] Pracher was one of those pastors who utilized Haid's "remodeled" Rosary.[385] He reported that, "I thereby was able to get the people to be satisfied soon with three Our Fathers and Aves, and finally even with just one and with the Apostles Creed."[386] Thus did some Aufklärung Catholics attempt to make Marian prayer both scriptural and an act of the understanding as well as the lips.

25. Conclusion

Thus it can be seen at least in part that the attempts at liturgical reform by Aufklärung Catholics were extremely broad and thorough-going, and that they met with a great deal of success, particularly in Southwestern Germany and part of the Rhineland. Aufklärung Catholics attempted to eliminate the mechanical character of worship; they stressed the instructional and morally motivating aspect of liturgy, put most of the liturgy in the vernacular, promoted congregational participation and congregational singing, placed the reading of the Scriptures and preaching at the center of the eucharistic celebration, eliminated the saying of Mass when a congregation was not present, re-oriented church architecture, improved the Scripture readings in the Missal, criticized the overstress of the Masses for the dead, worked for the elimination of Mass stipends, toned down devotion to the saints and Mary and required fasting, stopped simultaneous Masses, strove to eradicate superstitious and quasi-superstitious practices, attempted to make Baptism, Penance, and Confirmation more meaningful to the people and re-vitalize the Ritual, called and worked for reform of the Breviary and the legalistically mandatory recitation of it by priests.

In almost every one of these areas what Aufklärung Catholics advocated and enacted has been again advocated and enacted by Vatican II and post-conciliar liturgical reforms.[387] It is almost as if the latter copied from the textbook of the former.

Perhaps much of the Aufklärung movement of liturgical reform can be best summed up in the words of Wessenberg himself when, at the end of his administration of the diocese of Constance he wrote to his much beloved clergy: "Beloved brothers, colleagues, and friends in the Lord! When I review with calm earnestness the twenty-five years during which it was given to me to provide leadership for your struggles and efforts, it gives me a great deal of inner joy to be able to publicly bear an honorable witness to you that the condition of pastoral care has within that period of time improved itself immensely in many regards. The public veneration of God has received a more worthy form, a greater seriousness and order," particularly through "the spread of a general song and devotion book . . . the preaching of the Divine Word has been brought into closer relationship again to the holy sacrifice of the Mass, as was the original intention and order of the Church." The parish worship service as the common bond has been promoted and thus "has the worthy celebration of the Sundays and Holy Days essentially improved. . . . By means of Vesper devotions in the vernacular, congregational church prayers, litanies and hymns, by the reading aloud of appropriate portions of the Scripture during afternoon devotions and prayer hours and processions, the soul-killing mechanical spirit has been confronted and the spirit and heart has been raised up in inner, joyful and edifying adoration. . . . The salutary reception of the Sacraments of Penance and the Eucharist has been effectively fostered by appropriate liturgical celebrations. . . . This is particularly so in the case of the celebration of the Eucharist for children. . . . Likewise in the administration of the other holy Sacraments the understanding and power of edification of the ecclesiastical rites and ceremonies has received a certain happy increase . . . because they were administered with appropriate German instructions, prayers and hymns. . . . Live up to your high calling . . . do everything fo the sake of the Gospel, hold fast and unshakably onto that costly treasure, the Faith delivered to the Church, which has been entrusted to you! Listen to and love accordingly the Church as loyal, teachable children who with the greatest certitude walk with their hands in that of their loving mother!"[388]

These do not sound like the words of a rebellious son of the Catholic Church who for many years led an unchurchly and ungodly revolution in liturgical and other reforms, as Wessenberg has most often been described. The hundreds and hundreds of priests who had worked under his leadership for a quarter of a century did not view him that way, as was evidenced in the deep-felt expressions of gratitude and affection that were forthcoming from the clergy from almost all of the Chapters throughout his diocese.[389] On a larger scale basically the same thing is also true of the general Aufklärung attempts at liturgical reform: They were for the most part undertaken sincerely, and highly regarded by large numbers of clergy and laity of the time.

2. AUFKLÄRUNG CATHOLICISM OVERVIEW

Obviously the Aufklärung Catholics of late eighteenth and early nineteenth century Germany were not concerned only with the reform of the liturgy, important as they thought that was. Their Weltanschauung mandated reform in practically every area of life, sacred and secular. Within the confines of a single monograph it is of course not possible to describe as thoroughly these other reforms as the liturgical reforms have been. Nevertheless, for the sake of perspective it is important to provide at least an outline of the other major reform efforts of Aufklärung Catholics.

1. *Enlightenment Stress on the Bible*

The Enlightenment has the reputation of making a rather simplistic concept of man's reason into the standard against which all things were to be measured. However, for Aufklärung Catholics the stress on reason did not mean the elimination of the belief in God's revelation as manifested through the Scriptures. In fact, as we have seen somewhat in the area of the liturgy, Aufklärung Catholics stressed very strongly the importance of the Bible. However they stressed the need to get at the literal sense of the Bible, rather than the mystical or allegorical senses which were so very often popular in previous times. Consequently they also felt that it was very necessary to see to it that priests received a thorough grounding in Scriptural studies during their seminary training. How else could they fulfill one of their main functions, namely, that of preaching on the Scriptures at the eucharistic celebration? But the Aufklärung Catholics did not stop at placing the Bible once more prominently in the hands of the priests. They also promoted the reading of the Bible very widely among the laity.[390] Here too the Aufklärung Catholics sound very much like Vatican II Catholics.

2. *Catechetical and Educational Reforms*

The first part of the nineteenth century stood at the brink of the Age of the Masses. The great mass education systems had not yet been established, but they were in the offing, with the work of such pioneers as Pestalozzi at their bases. Logically following their notion that the liturgy was to instruct and motivate and that for the same purposes the Bible was to be widely distributed and employed, Aufklärung Catholics promoted mass education with all possible vigor, both through the churches and secular politics. Naturally also Aufklärung Catholics brought their concern for an improvement and spread

53

of education in general to the very crucial matter of religious education, or catechetics. Heinrich von Wessenberg, for example, insisted that his priests not only preach at the Eucharist but also give religious instructions outside Mass on a regular and frequent basis. Wessenberg also personally saw to it that his seminarians not only had regular instructions and experience in preaching during their seminary days but also in religious teaching. He was a close friend of Pestalozzi himself and did everything he could to promote his new ideas and techniques. Wessenberg and other Aufklärung theologians also wrote new catechisms. To promote this enterprise in his own diocese Wessenberg offered prizes for the best catechisms written; he found many takers. Arrangements were made to give special instructions in the new catechetical techniques to priests already in the field. The status of the teacher was raised and priests were cautioned to relinquish their clerical privilege and to become "a friend of the teacher." Like contemporary Catholics, who are experiencing a catechetical renewal, Aufklärung Catholics also placed great stress on the vital importance of religious instruction, updating the training of the priests and teachers in theology in general but most particularly in the areas of biblical studies and in the study of church history and the history of doctrines and the employment of the latest techniques of education.[391]

3. *Theological Reform*

Aufklärung Catholics, as their name indicates, felt that new light needed to be shed on the area of theology, making use of the best of contemporary philosophical thought. Consequently they were very critical of Scholasticism, or what at least passed for Scholasticism at that time. Although for the most part the majority of Aufklärung churchmen engaged in what they considered to be practical reforms rather than doctrinal reforms, a number of teachings were very widely criticized by them. Indulgences, for example, were often thought to be conducive to superstition and hence to be eliminated. The devil came in for a particularly hard time and was most often transformed into a sort of mythical personification of evil in the abstract. Hence, for example, the exorcism in the administration of Baptism as found in Wessenberg's new Ritual was directed against evil rather than the devil as a person.[392] Some Aufklärung churchmen, such as Father Benedict Werkmeister, stated that the doctrine of transubstantiation was not one that Catholics were bound to hold (this stance anticipated the work of the contemporary Catholic theologians Schoonenberg and Schillebeeckx, and others, who developed similar positions, by some 150 years).

Besides the churchmen of the Aufklärung, who were mostly interested in practical church reforms, there were several academic theologians who strove for the reform of theology in the Aufklärung spirit. The case of the early Johann Adam Möhler (before 1828, when the anti-celibacy movement appeared to be the rock on which his reform spirit, if not broke at least bent very badly) was mentioned above, as well as that of Johannes Baptist

Hirscher, whose area of focus was moral and pastoral theology. But there were three more philosophical theologians who undertook a theoretical approach to theology in the spirit of the Aufklärung, of reason and reform. One was Bernard Bolzano (1781-1848), who taught Religionswissenschaft at the University of Prague the first two decades of the nineteenth century until he was removed in 1821. Bolzano, who was also an outstanding theoretical mathematician, developed pioneer philosophical directions in linguistic analysis, philosophy of religion, and social ethics. He narrowly escaped being placed on the Index by name and being suspended (years-long efforts by supporters and timely deaths of enemies saved him), and continued throughout his life to be a power for reform in Austrian Catholicism through his disciples, his scholarly work and his correspondence.[393]

A second theoretical theologian imbued with the Aufklärung spirit was Georg Hermes (1775-1831). He was appointed Professor of Theology at the University of Münster in 1807, and at the new University of Bonn in 1820. All his scholarly efforts were bent toward putting a thoroughly rational foundation under Catholic theology. In this he was supported by Baron Spiegel, the Archbishop of Cologne; his teaching and writings earned him very many followers who were quickly appointed to professorships: "Like the theological faculty at Bonn, to which only pupils of Hermes had been appointed since 1826 (Archterfeldt, Braun, Vogelsang, Müller), the seminary at Cologne and a large part of the clergy were soon imbued with his ideas. Even the other faculties of Bonn included followers of his, particularly, Professor Clement August von Droste-Hülshoff in law and Elvenich in philosophy. In a very short time the theological faculties of Breslau, Münster and Braunsberg, the seminary at Trier, many cathedral chapters and instructorships in religion at the gymnasia were filled with Hermensians. . . . Achterfeldt and Siemers wrote for use in the higher schools textbooks of religious instructions incorporating his views. . . . The Archbishop of Cologne, Baron von Spiegel, continued to champion Hermesianism even after the death of its author, and he silenced by repeated favorable reports the doubts that had been awakened in Rome as to the correctness of the new doctrine."[394] The archbishop died in 1835 (upon which "Pope Gregory XVI piously remarked, 'Hence it is fortunate that this archbishop is dead, who at any rate was basically a bad bishop.'"[395]) and a few weeks later a thoroughgoing condemnation of Hermes' works was issued by Rome. Spiegel's successor, the very conservative and authoritarian Clement August von Droste Vischering (an early personal foe of Hermes), rammed through an elimination of all the disciples and influences of Hermes within his jurisdiction, and even beyond.

The third theoretical theologian who worked to reform theology in the spirit of the Aufklärung and reason (though with strong influences of idealistic philosophy) was Anton Günther (1783-1863), who lived most of his life in Vienna. He too gained a large following among Catholic academic philosophers and theologians all across Austria and Germany. But Günther's work also fell before the condemnation of the Congregation of the Index, in 1857 for a variety of reasons, but particularly, as Pope Pius IX himself wrote, because of its "fundamental rationalism, which is the controlling factor of his philosophy even in the handling of Christian dogmas."[396] Many of Günther's followers joined the Old Catholic Church when it was formed in opposition to the dogma of papal infallibility declared in 1870.

4. *Ecumenism*

When the history of the ecumenical movement is recounted it is most often stated that it began with the world missionary conference at Edinburgh in 1910. Earlier roots in the nineteenth century are of course also traced and sometimes a nod is given in the direction of the exchange of letters between the Protestant thinker Leibniz and Bishop Bossuet in the latter part of the seventeenth century. However, with the exception of a Catholic or two here or there, such as Bishop Bossuet, the participation of the Roman Catholic Church in ecumenism is usually said to have begun in Germany shortly after the First World War. However here too the Aufklärung Catholics of Germany again are overlooked. For example, just 130 years before John XXIII announced the calling of Vatican II to renew the Church so as to be ready for Christian reunion, Father Fridolin Huber wrote that he and his many colleagues were working vigorously for reform within the Roman Catholic Church not only for its own sake but also in the hope that through the elimination of the glaring defects within the Catholic Church the reasons for the division between Catholics and Protestants would thereby disappear. Indeed even some forty years before that the Aufklärung Catholic prince *par excellence*, Emperor Joseph II of Austria, also felt that as the Catholic Church was purified Protestants would reunite with it in corporate fashion. Vatican II's second great ecumenical document, the "Declaration on Religious Liberty," was also anticipated by the Aufklärung Catholics in their constant insistence on religious freedom and freedom of conscience. This religious freedom was also extended by them specifically to Jews, a freedom not yet fully enjoyed by Jews today in Roman Catholic Spain, but legislated in Vatican II's decree on Non-Christian religions.

In ecumenism the Aufklärung Catholics most naturally were primarily concerned with Protestants. At a time when Roman Catholic churchmen were still writing of Martin Luther as something akin to the devil incarnate we find that a number of Aufklärung churchmen and theologians exhibited a great deal of sympathy for Luther in his concern for, and attempt to reform, the Catholic Church. One of the Catholic Aufklärung reformers even promoted a very ambitious plan for the reunion of the Catholic and Protestant Churches. He suggested that Catholic and Protestant congregations alternately use the same place of worship and that they also have an exchange of preachers so that they might hear about each other's beliefs and practices in an authentic, irenic manner. Eventually they would develop a kind of joint liturgical community and eventually this road would lead to unity. Werkmeister, the author of this plan, was able to put some of these ideas into action, although in a very limited fashion, in Stuttgart where he was one of the court chaplains. It was the same Werkmeister who was able to arrange to bring Protestant and Catholic religion teachers and also Protestant and Catholic clergy together to study the education methods of Pestalozzi. In commenting on what he had already accomplished in this joint Catholic and Protestant study Werkmeister rejoiced that the barriers between the confessions were coming down to some extent and hoped that they would continue to do so. Such joint Protestant and Catholic endeavors in the religious field deepened as the century developed. In the 1830's a theological journal was founded by clergymen, aimed at both Protestant and Catholic clerics, with the editorial team being made up of both Protestant and Catholic clergymen. The new hymnbooks produced by Aufklärung Catholics also reflected the more open attitude toward Protestantism in that they now freely borrowed from Protestant hymnbooks as well as older Catholic ones.[397]

5. *Mixed Marriage*

The question of mixed marriage was as vexing a problem a hundred and fifty years ago as at present. Aufklärung Catholics felt that to take the rigid Catholic stand on mixed marriage, that is, that all the children must be raised in the Catholic Church, was, among other things, destructive of the possibility of church reunion. They also felt that such an insistence on the Catholic side was a basic violation of justice and the conscience of the Protestant partner. They even went to the length of feeling that such mixed marriages entered into in the proper spirit would provide the seeds of religious freedom and respect. Von Wessenberg even saw to it that in his diocese both the Protestant and Catholic clergymen would be involved in the mixed marriage ceremony, namely, the marriage ceremony was always first performed before the minister of the bridegroom and then afterwards before the minister of the bride. But in many other instances the marriage ceremony was conducted jointly by the two clergymen.[398]

6. *Restructuring Papal Government*

Aufklärung Catholics realized that basic changes in the structure of the Catholic Church were necessary to put through far-reaching reforms. This stress on structural changes was a particularly central theme in the work and writings of the long-lived von Wessenberg, who was active from the beginning of the century until after the mid-century mark. These structure reform efforts by him and other Aufklärung Catholics earned them the ire of the Vatican. To this day Wessenberg's reputation has been so maligned that he is almost never heard of by Roman Catholics, and when he is, it is usually in denigrating fashion. The same is true of Werkmeister and other of the Aufklärung theologians and churchmen. It is not merely that their values were held in disdain by contemporary conservatives but that quite incredible lies were told about them.[399]

In response of course the Aufklärung Catholics filled their writing with the severest criticisms of Rome, particularly of the Curia and curialist theology and tactics of domination. The earlier mentioned papal encyclical *Mirari vos* issued in 1832 delivered the *coup de grace* to budding liberal Catholicism in France, but it met with a bitter reaction and criticism from the German Aufklärung Catholics.[400] Aufklärung Catholics felt very strongly that the claims and pretentions of Rome should be vastly scaled down, that the papal office was to be one of unity rather than authoritarian domination. The role of the bishop vis-à-vis Rome was to be one of much greater independence, and much greater stress was placed on the bishops of individual nations acting together in joint fashion[401] (not unlike the way post-Vatican II national episcopal conferences do).

7. *The "Synodal Movement"*

However, Aufklärung Catholics were not content with scaling down the power claims of Rome in favor of the bishop; they also wished to eliminate the authoritarian claims of power on the part of the bishop as well. Aufklärung Catholics wanted all of the elements within the Church to participate in the decision-making of the Church. Hence, they argued that the bishop should act conjointly with his presbyterium of clergy, and that associations or conferences of clergy should be set up to meet regularly, and that diocesan synods made up of lay and clerical representatives of the whole diocese ought to be called to help decide the most pressing questions of the day.[402] In sum, Aufklärung Catholics promoted a great deal more freedom and responsibility for *all* elements within the Church. A whole series of petitions for synodal governments were organized in Southwest Germany in the 1830's and 40's, known throughout Germany as the "synodal movement." (Today in Catholic Church history writings, however, one can hardly find a mention of it, even though it produced a number of new titles for the Index of Forbidden Books.)[403]

It is interesting to note that as a strong countermovement developed in the 1830's and 40's on the wave of a general cultural backlash the Aufklärung Catholics were strongly criticized by their opponents as being "unchurchly." In fact, the anti-Aufklärung movement was known then and subsequently by conservative Catholic writers as the "churchly" movement, *die kirchliche Bewegung*. When one looks carefully at what these writers both then and since meant by *kirchlich*, it is clear that the touchstone was whether or not a person spoke and acted totally in favor of authoritarian government in the hands of the bishop and the Vatican.

8. *Clerical Celibacy*

In the 1820's and particularly in the 1830's there was an extraordinarily strong movement to lift the law of mandatory clerical celibacy with a flood of literature on the subject, a great deal of support on the part of educated laymen, and most importantly, on the part of huge numbers of priests and theologians. In the diocese of Freiburg in Southwestern Germany alone a number of petitions over a several-year period were sent in, sometimes to the archbishop and sometimes even to the state legislature, which at that time had a great deal to do with Church affairs. One such petition in the early 1840's was signed by over 600 of the diocesan clergy in the diocese of Freiburg, more than two-thirds of the secular clergy in that diocese. The entire Catholic theology faculty of the University of Freiburg supported the lifting of mandatory clerical celibacy, and did so both in their individual writings and publications and also in the signing of petitions.[404]

9. Secular Moral Issues

Aufklärung Catholics were concerned not only with internal reform of the Catholic Church but also with the current moral issues, which they felt included the need for a great deal more freedom and responsibility in the political spheres, that is, such things as freedom of the press, freedom of speech, freedom of assembly, representative government, promotion of education. Quite naturally the area of moral concern for the Aufklärung Catholics also included those centering on sex, as for example priestly celibacy. The problem of divorce and remarriage was very much discussed by Aufklärung Catholics and they clearly came down on the side of the need for allowing divorce and remarriage where marriage has been a failure.[405]

10. The Extent and Variety of Aufklärung Catholicism

The greatest stronghold of Aufklärung Catholicism was the diocese of Constance, since the seventh century the largest diocese in area and population in Germany. It included Southwestern Germany and the great majority of German-speaking Switzerland, extending from the Rhine on the west, the St. Gotthard pass on the south, the Iller River on the east up through Ulm, Gmünd and across the Neckar river north of Marbach. In 1435 the diocese had 17,060 priests, 1760 parishes and 350 monasteries and convents. There were many losses in the Reformation, but in 1750 there were still 3,774 secular priests, 2,764 monks, 3,147 nuns and a Catholic population of 891,948.[406] In 1805, when Wessenberg took charge, there were "about one and a half million Catholics, about a third of whom were in Baden. The total clergy numbered 6,608 persons, including 2,365 secular priests, for the most part employed in the care of souls or teaching, 1,220 non-mendicant monks, 906 from different mendicant orders, and 2,117 nuns. There were therefore 233 persons per cleric!"[407]

In reading over the literature of the first part of the nineteenth century one finds that the great majority of the clergy of Southwestern Germany, the entire Catholic theology faculty of the University of Freiburg, almost half of the Catholic theologians of the University of Tübingen, in Württemberg, the majority of the Catholic theology faculty of the University of Bonn, and many other Catholic theologians elsewhere in Germany and Austria were judged Aufklärung Catholics at the beginning of the 1830's. The same is true also of the rector of the seminary in Southwestern Germany, as well as the director of the teacher-training institution in Southwestern Germany, also the vast majority of the grammar and high school teachers and very many of the journalists and publishers. Hence in the beginning of the 1830's the intellectual, educational and clerical communities were overwhelmingly Aufklärung Catholics, at least in Southwestern Germany and also in many other areas of German-speaking lands. Moreover, there was at least a certain amount of mutual support and collaboration in the reform efforts of Aufklärung Catholics in various parts of the Germanies.[408]

One twentieth-century German scholar antagonistic to the Aufklärung, Ferdinand Strobel, granted that the extent of the spread of the spirit of the Aufklärung among the common folk is difficult to gauge, and then referred to an earlier scholar as arguing that "only from around 1830 on were the majority of the people completely taken up by the Aufklärung. He therefore places the highpoint of the Aufklärung between 1830 and 1850."[409] Strobel, in speaking of Baden, nevertheless argued that much of the common folk were opposed to the Aufklärung in church matters even though they "were corrupted by political liberalism" in political matters. No persuasive evidence is provided, however, especially in view of his admission of all the strengths of the Aufklärung listed above, including "until 1840 the majority of the clergy still declared for the Aufklärung," and even went so far as to state that "the majority of *Volksschule* teachers appeared to be the source of radicalism."[410] If all that is true, it is difficult to see how the Aufklärung could not have had a significant influence on the general population—which was taught and led for so many years by these clergy, teachers, etc.

Hermann Lauer makes just this differentiated point: "Wessenberg's reforms were received very differently by the Catholic *Volk*. The *aufgeklärte* circles of the cities received Wessenberg enthusiastically and praised his merits to the stars. The reforms also found a favorable reception with a part of the country people, that is, where an otherwise diligent pastor concerned about school and undertakings helpful to the community knew how to present them in a favorable light. But another part of the people anguished under them. They could not understand why all of a sudden the old handed down religious customs should be tossed into the waste basket. They persistently resisted the reforms and vigorously opposed the reform clergy. . . . Finally, however, the opposition of the people in most places was overcome."[411]

As noted earlier the reform movement among Aufklärung Catholics in the first half of the nineteenth century in Germany was not uniform. There were some extreme left elements among the reform movements, although usually not as extreme as they have often been painted by conservative Catholic churchmen and historians. But by far the vast majority of the Aufklärung Catholics were what might be described accurately as moderate reformers, that is, they wished to reform the Roman Catholic Church; they very definitely rejected the idea of breaking with it. When, for example, in the middle 1840's a small group of leftwing Catholics broke away to form what was known as "German Catholicism," they were for the most part rejected by Aufklärung Catholics, with one of their great leaders, von Wessenberg, in the forefront of this rejection.[412]

It should be clear, at least in outline fashion, that Vatican II and post-Vatican II Liberal Catholicism had an extraordinary way a predecessor in Aufklärung Catholicism, not only in the reform of the liturgy, but also in the stress on the Bible, the development of ecumenism, catechetical reform, critiques of dogmas with the use of contemporary thought, severe criticism of centralized authoritarianism, particuarly curialism, and authoritarian episcopal power, the promotion of synodal and democratic government, the emphasizing of the importance of the laity, the rethinking of many moral problems such as freedom and responsibility, celibacy, mixed marriages, and divorce. Moreover, in some areas, particularly in Southwestern Germany, Aufklärung Catholicism had the support of the great majority of the theologians, the clergy, the teachers, and the educated laity. In short, it had the support basically of every level of society except that of the bishopric and Rome. So long as Wessenberg was the Administrator of the diocese of Constance, from 1802 to 1827, even one bishopric was on its side.

11. The Demise of Aufklärung Catholicism

However, Rome saw to it first of all that Wessenberg was never consecrated a bishop, and hence it was possible to have him removed from his position as Administrator in 1827. But even before that, Rome gradually restricted his area of influence by breaking up and diminishing in size the diocese of Constance in several operations. In 1814 the large Swiss district was removed from the diocese and in 1817, after the death of the Bishop, von Dalberg, the Bavaria and Württemberg districts were also removed; in 1821 the diocese was totally dissolved and attached to the newly erected archdiocese of Freiburg in Breisgau—though this latter move could not be implemented until 1827 when the state of Baden allowed Wessenberg to be removed as Administrator of the diocese of Constance. Clearly most of this dismemberment was designed to cut away all diocesan control of Wessenberg (at each step of the way Wessenberg's name was proposed as bishop, but each time it was rejected by the Vatican, at times with great protracted battles).

Hence in 1830, although Aufklärung Catholics did not have the support of any episcopal seen in Southwestern Germany, or anywhere else for that matter, they did seem to have the upper hand on other levels; yet by 1842 all eight of the Aufklärung Catholics that made up the Catholic theology faculty of the University of Freiburg in 1830 were eliminated by one sort of intrigue or another.[413] Conservatives were placed in the positions of rectors of seminaries and directors of the teacher-training institutions. As a result, by the latter part of the 1840's the conservative elements in Roman Catholicism were priding themselves on the great triumphs that they were enjoying. The new priests that were being turned out were *kirchlich*, that is, authoritarian, in their attitudes; the same was true of the new teachers being trained. The many Aufklärung journals and newspapers that flourished in the early 1830's had pretty well dried up and disappeared by 1850.[414] New Rituals being put into use were marked by the ever greater use of Latin. The general result was that if one were to compare the Catholicism of 1855 with the Catholicism of 25 years earlier the difference would have been like night and day. Aufklärung Catholicism seemed to have been almost entirely obliterated in a short time after it appeared to have an unbreakable hold on what one would think were nine-tenths of the key areas.

12. *Reflection On the Anti-Aufklärung Attack*

A reflective remark is in order at this point. Given the facts that the memory of Aufklärung Catholicism was at first most hostilely attacked and then almost wiped by the near silence of subsequent Catholic church historians, and given the restored image of Aufklärung Catholicism of the preceding pages that looks so extraordinarily like Vatican II Catholicism, certain questions naturally arise: Were there no plausible grounds on which the opponents of Aufklärung Catholicism based their opposition? Does it not border on the incredible that so many highly placed responsible Catholic ecclesiastical leaders, theologians, and historians could have taken actions so distorting and suppressive of facts?

Clearly the majority of the opponents of Aufklärung Catholicism very likely were not evil men, men of "bad will"—though one must not totally discount Lord Acton's dictum about power corrupting and absolute power corrupting absolutely. However, security is a basic human need. To attain and retain it myriads of institutions are developed and preserved. When a wide range of the fundamental institutions of a society are suddenly threatened, the involuntary reaction of most people, including, or rather, especially, most leaders is fear and forceful reestablishment of the tottering institutions.

The end of the eighteenth century and first portion of the nineteenth century saw just such a profound shaking of many of the taken-for-granted institutions of Christendom. Already during the eighteenth-century Enlightenment in France (though *not* in Germany) the Catholic Church was attacked from many sides under the banner of liberty. During the French Revolution, with its slogan of *liberté, fraternité, egalité,* the Church was tremendously ravaged—and not merely on the physical level. Priests and religious were persecuted, exiled, and murdered. Church property was desecrated—some being rededicated to the goddess of reason—and confiscated all over France and Central Europe. The situation was only somewhat amelioriated by Napoleon—the same Napoleon who kidnapped and browbeat Pope Pius VII. But the Church's troubles were only just starting. The movement of democratic liberalism in its wider nineteenth-century sense cut away at the very foundation of the authoritarian, hierarchical structure of the Church and of society in general. This was followed by the more perverse movement of Socialism, which would destroy the very basis of society—and hence the Church—that is, private property. And as if this were not enough, there then came the satanic development of Communism—the embodiment of materialism and atheism. Add to this the fact that the period between 1815 and 1870 was constantly filled with revolutions all over Europe and North and South America, the development of anarchism, scientism, evolutionism, and Protestant "liberal theology" with its debunking of the Bible as a Jesus myth foisted upon humanity by a dozen Jewish fishermen, and one will begin to see why so many nineteenth-century Catholics were in a panic. Nothing seemed certain; nothing seemed stable anymore. Everything appeared to be washed away in the deluge of revolution and isms that swept across nineteenth-century Europe. In terror people frantically searched for something stable. Many Catholics found it in an authoritarian Church with its structured-from-above hierarchy and the papacy at its apex. The cry among many seemed to be, "To Peter, to the Rock!" An impenetrable bastion was built around the Rock fortress, and the condemned world was shut out. Until better times would come, only invectives and sallies were to come forth from the Rock.

It was within this context that the fearful opponents of Aufklärung Catholics viewed their reform efforts. Of course there were extreme, reductionist notions advocated by some Aufklärung Catholics, as for example, Theiner (though in fact they were amazingly few, as indicated in the above pages). But the presence of such relatively extreme elements cannot possibly explain the extraordinarily strong reaction that developed against this basically reforming, not revolutionary, movement. Every movement of any magnitude, conservative or liberal, will have its relatively extreme elements. But the overwhelming crescendo of the Catholic anti-Aufklärung forces in the 1830's and following can be understood only within the broader cultural context of political, social, and intellectual reaction. That was the Age of Meternich, the Age of the Holy Alliance of the Prussian, Russian, and Austrian Emperors reacting against the Jacobins, Decembrists, and Garbibaldi's Red Shirts. In Catholicism it was also the Age of Gregory XVI and Pius IX, of *Mirari vos*, The Syllabus of Errors, and Papal Infallibility.

Even granting the fear, at times panic, of the men of the Establishment, there is still the question of whether they could have been responsible for such gross condemnations of Aufklärung Catholicism, of such totally black and white distinctions, of such complete assumptions of the insincerity and even evil of Aufklärung Catholics. No systematic attempt has been made in this study to provide representative quotations of the vilification of the Aufklärung Catholic reformers, nor will the space be taken to do so now. It will be sufficient, I believe, to allude to the leadership given the opponents of reforming efforts in Catholicism by the papacy.

In 1832, early in his sixteen-year long pontificate, Pope Gregory XVI made it clear that the "reform" of the Catholic Church was not even something to be desired, let alone tolerated or encouraged: "It is obviously absurd and injurious to her [the Catholic Church] to demand some kind of 'restoration and regeneration' as necessary for her existence and growth—as if it were possible for her to be subject to defect, to decay, or other such deficiencies."[415]

Forgetting the gospel saying, "Whoever is not against you is for you" (Luke 9:50), and remembering only the other saying, "Whoever is not for me is against me" (Luke 11:23), Gregory XVI saw the world around him as full of evil men attacking the Church he was leading: "Brazen immorality, impudent knowledge, dissolute license abound. Holy things are despised, and the majesty of divine worship, which possesses both great power and great necessity, is attacked and polluted by malevolent men, and made a matter of ridicule. Correct doctrine is perverted and errors of all kinds are insolently disseminated. Neither the Church's laws, rights, institutions, nor the holiest matters of discipline are safe from the audacity of men speaking evil . . . in an abominable manner, the schools disseminate monstrous opinions, by which the Catholic faith is no longer impugned occultly and stealthily, but horrific and deadly war is waged against it openly and everywhere. Through the instruction and example of teachers, after the minds of the youth have been corrupted, immense harm to religion and unutterable immorality has resulted . . . . This accumulation of misfortunes must be sought in the first place in the malice and bad will of those societies into which whatever is sacrilegious, opprobrious and blasphemous in the various heresies and criminal sects has flowed as if into a sewer, full of all uncleanness. These things, venerable brethren, and many others besides, perhaps even graver, which it would take too long at this time to enumerate (and which you already know), beset us with excruciating and unceasing pain."[416]

Did Aufklärung Catholics fall into the category "malevolent men" for the Pope (and like-minded lesser clerics)? Church historians have usually interpreted this encyclical *Mirari vos* as primarily aimed at Lamennais and his reforming Catholic followers in France, and doubtless part of it was so oriented, especially the condemnation of the separation of Church and state. But significant portions of it were obviously composed with Aufklärung Catholicism in mind as well, and in some instances exclusively. The references above about despising holy things and attacking and ridiculing the majesty of divine worship were clearly aimed (and almost exclusively) at the liturgical reforms outlined in this study. So too the statements about schools disseminating monstrous opinions and teachers giving corrupting examples were directed, even if not exclusively, at the wide penetration of Aufklärung reform ideas throughout much of the school system including the universities in Catholic Germany that has been only briefly described in these pages. In addition, *Mirari vos* contains a long paragraph condemning efforts at allowing divorce in failed marriages—in which efforts many Aufklärung Catholics shared.

One of the goals of Aufklärung Catholicism—again, mentioned only briefly in this study—was the elimination of mandatory celibacy for priests. The movement reached large public proportions in southwestern Germany at the time of the Encyclical and was clearly aimed at directly by Gregory XVI: "At this point we desire to call upon your constancy for holy religion against the vile attack on clerical celibacy. You know that it is growing by the day, thanks to the collusion of the most depraved philosophers of our time and some of the ecclesiastical orders who, unmindful of their person and their duty, are borne away by the allurements of pleasure. They have gone so far as to dare to direct public and, in some places, repeated demands to the rulers of the abolition of that most sacred point of discipline. But we are ashamed to speak at length of these base attempts."417

Still another charge pointed directly, and just about solely, at the reform movement in Germany was what today would be called ecumenism, but by the Pope was labelled "indifferentism": "And now we must mention another fruitful cause of evil by which the Church is afflicted at present, namely, indifferentism—or that vicious manner of thinking, which mushrooms on all sides owing to the wiles of malicious men and which holds that the soul's eternal salvation can be obtained by the profession of any faith, provided a man's morals are good and decent."418

From that position it was but an easy step to the suppression of the freedom of thought and speech: "Now from this evil-smelling spring of indifferentism flows the erroneous and absurd opinion—or rather, madness [*deliramentum*]—that freedom of conscience must be asserted and vindicated for everyone. This most pestilential error opens the door to the complete and immoderate liberty of opinions, which works such widespread harm both in Church and state . . . . Thence proceeds transformation of minds, corruption of youth, a contempt among the people for the Church, for sacred things and laws. In one word, that pestilence is more threatening to the public weal than any other, since as experience shows, or as is known from antiquity, kingdoms which flourished by reason of wealth, of rule, and of glory perished because of this sole evil: the immoderate liberty of opinions, license of speech, and the penchant for novelties."419

This condemnation of freedom of thought and speech doubtless struck other reform-minded Catholics than those in Germany, but obviously also included them in a central way. So too did the condemnation of the freedom of the press, for as often seen in the above pages, Catholic Germany was full of reform-oriented books, newspapers, journals, and pamphlets: "Here reference must be made that deleterious liberty, which can never be execrated and detested sufficiently, of printing and of publishing writings of every kind, which some dare to demand and to promote with such insolence. We are struck with horror, venerable brethren, when we see with what portentous errors we are oppressed. They are spread far and wide by a multitude of books, pamphlets, and other writings, small indeed in size but very great in malice, from which comes that curse spread across the earth that we bewail."[420]

Bearing in mind that Gregory's reign from 1830 to 1846 was followed by Pius IX's from 1846 to 1878 (Pius IX repeated all these condemnations of Gregory's in his 1864 Syllabus of Errors, in which he finally condemned this proposition: "The Roman Pontiff can, and ought to, reconcile himself to, and agree with, progress, liberalism, and modern civilization,")[421] it is quite credible that opponents of Aufklärung Catholicism could have launched an indiscriminate and obliterating attack on it. The conspiracy mentality which sees things totally in black and white needs little justification in facts to issue blanket condemnations; if that was true of these two popes, it was *a fortiori* also true of their like-minded followers.

3. CONTEMPORARY COMMENTARY

As noted at the beginning of this study, the first task of an historian is to describe and analyze his subject as accurately as possible within its own time frame—even though the motivation for the particular study was in some way promoted by the historian's own cultural context. That task has been undertaken in the preceding pages. Beyond that the historian may also properly essay other tasks, such as, compare attitudes, ideas, events, etc. from two different periods. That was also done here, simply noting the similarity, or lack thereof, between Aufklärung Catholicism and Vatican II Catholicism; no attempt was made to show a causal connection between the two, for all signs pointed away from any such nexus.

But, having found an extraordinary similarity between Aufklärung Catholicism and Vatican II Catholicism, a whole series of intriguing questions present themselves to the historian, and beyond that to the theologian of today. I will analyze and comment briefly on only those questions I as historian and as contemporary theologian judge to be of most pressing importance.

First it should be noted that with all the likenesses between Aufklärung Catholicism and Vatican II Catholicism, there are also some very important differences, found mostly in theology, church-state relations, and the level of promulgation of the reforms. In contemporary Catholic theology there is not such a heavy weight placed on the role of abstract reason by itself (particularly as found in Hermesianism). Moreover, in the last 150 years there have been extraordinary advances especially in the sense of the importance of history and symbolism, in psychology, biblical studies and philosophical analysis— though one should not underestimate the historical research of Wessenberg nor the philosophical investigations of Bolzano (especially his four-volume *Wissenschaftslehre* in 1837). In church-state relations the position of reform-minded Catholics of 1827 and 1977 are diametrically opposite. Aufklärung Catholics saw the state as one of the most effective instruments of bringing about reform within the Catholic Church because for the most part the various German states, Protestant and Catholic, were sympathetically inclined. Contemporary reform-minded Catholics, however, find the state too often an instrument of oppression or reaction (whether left or right) and hence have followed the banner of liberalism and French Liberal Catholicism (Lammenais and Montelambert) in this regard.

But the most significant difference is that many of the basic reforms of the two eras were legislated on a world level, at least in principle, at Vatican II.

67

There is no doubt that this is a massively important advance beyond Aufklärung Catholicism. It is like the difference between getting an advanced guard plus a few divisions turned around, and getting the whole army faced in a new direction. Caution should be observed, however, since there is still a great distance to go after turning an army around, important as that is, before arriving at the destination. The Council of Constance (1414-1418) and its aftermath is proof that getting basic reform decrees passed in an ecumenical council and working at their implementation for a few, or even many, years does not necessarily ensure effective, lasting reform. Here was a Council, reckoned as "ecumenical" by the most conservative Roman Catholic traditionalists, which clearly declared that the Church gathered in ecumenical council was ultimately superior to the papacy (the Council proved this in deed by either persuading the then three contending popes to resign, or deposing them, and then electing a new pope, Martin V). Here too was a Council which decreed that from that time henceforth an ecumenical council should be held every ten years. Yet in a few years both of these decrees were totally disregarded: there were only five ecumenical councils called in the next 550 years; this 15th century "conciliar" period was followed first by that of the Renaissance papacy, then the Counter-Reformation papacy, and finally the papacy of Vatican I—in an evergrowing absolute papal power, which deliberately attacked the reform decrees of Constance.

Another important question that is prompted by the study of Aufklärung Catholicism is, why, after it had attained such extraordinary success and held so many key positions, was it almost totally obliterated in such a short time. Actually the reason is rather simple: Aufklärung Catholics were not able to accomplish a redistribution of power in the structure of the Catholic Church. This power of decision still lay almost entirely in the hands of the Pope and his curia and the bishops, who were picked by Rome. It was inevitable that a mistakenly appointed liberal bishop would die off, and be succeeded by a conservative one; the external forces temporarily restraining a conservative bishop, e.g., secular politics, public opinion, etc., would eventually shift in his favor. Then there was nothing that could protect the gains made by liberals from the conservative flood coming back in. This is what happened in the 1830's and subsequently.

The answer to this question can be put in another way, equally as simple: all final decision-making power continued to flow from the top down. For the first thousand years of Western Christianity much of the power flowed upward from below, especially exemplified in the widespread participation of priests and people in the selection of bishops.[422] But with the papal triumph in the struggle over the investiture of bishops in the eleventh century, more and more of the power flow was centered in the papacy, which gradually increased its powers of episcopal appointment. Efforts were made to reverse the tide, particularly in the conciliar movement of the early fifteenth century, which culminated in the reform ecumenical councils of Constance (1414) and Basel (1431); the latter ended in 1449 in total failure and the papacy reestablished its almost absolute decision-making authority. Another major attempt at reversing the flow of authority was made in the sixteenth-century Reformation. But the reformers soon found themselves outside the Roman Catholic Church, which by way of reaction was even more firmly forced into an authoritarian decision-from-above pattern for another two centuries. The movements of Gallicanism, Febronianism and even Josephinism in the eighteenth century tried in significant, though limited, ways to reverse the flow of power at the levels of the bishops and the national churches; their attempts at limited reforms met with even more limited success. Aufklärung Catholicism in the first part of the nineteenth century persisted in the reform effort and had the political insight in its later stages to strive for a more democratic synodal form of church decision-making, which would have fundamentally shifted the flow of power to a from below upward direction. A parallel effort was made in France at the same time and even in the United States with its election of bishops by the priests and lay trusteeism.[423]

But all these movements were swamped by a flood tide of Catholic conservatism, led by two of the most authoritarian, energetic and long-lived popes—Gregory XVI (1831–46) and Pius IX (1846–78). One more try was made at the end of the nineteenth century. It took different forms, from "Americanism" in the U.S., "democratizing priests" and what was later dubbed "Modernism" in France, *Reformkatholizismus* in Germany, and *Rinnovamento* in Italy. Among the many reforms advocated and to some extent undertaken in this complex of movements were efforts to redistribute power into the hands of the laity, priests and bishops, as well as the papacy.[424] These efforts and all reform attempts were absolutely crushed by the extremely vicious ecclesiastical terrorism initiated by the antimodernist papal decrees *Pascendi* and *Lamentabili* and the Oath Against Modernism in 1910.[425]

The pattern is clear: reform efforts have persistently had only ephemeral value and have finally failed because a shift in the flow of power to a from-below rather than from-above direction was never accomplished in a reform of the Catholic Church's power structure. The historian-theologian would have to conclude that if such a re-distribution of the loci of power in the Catholic Church is not accomplished in connection with the reforms of Vatican II, *all* of those reforms are likely to evaporate as did those of the Councils of Constance, Basel and subsequent reform movements like Aufklärung Catholicism, which vanished even from the pages of most of our history books.

NOTES

[1]Franz Schnabel, *Deutsche Geschichte im Neunzehnten Jahrhundert*, Vol. IV (Freiburg, 1951, 2nd ed.), pp. 10 ff.

[2]E.g., Adolf Rösch, *Das religiöse Leben in Hohenzollern unter dem Einflusse des Wessenbergianismus 1800-1850. Ein Beitrag zur Geschichte der religiösen Aufklärung in Süddeutschland.* Görres-Gesellschaft zur Pflege der Wissenschaft im katholischen Deutschland. Zweite Vereinsschrift für 1908 (Cologne, 1908); J.B. Sägmüller. *Wissenschaft und Glaube der kirchlichen Aufklärung (c. 1750-1850), (Essen, 1910)*; Georg May, *Inter-konfessionalismus in der ersten Hälfte des 19. Jahrhunderts* (Paderborn, 1969): "The powerful movement of the Aufklärung, which in Germany was dominant throughout the entire eighteenth century and the first decades of the nineteenth century, did not stop in front of the Catholic Church" (p. 9). Waldemar Trapp, *Vorgeschichte und Ursprung der liturgischen Bewegung* (Würzburg, 1939): "Timewise the moderate Aufklärung period cannot be precisely fixed. In general it extends somewhat later than the extreme type, running far into the Romantic [period—*in die Romantik*]. Its limitation must flow from the history of ideas. Still, some who came to the fore in their writing in the twenties and thirties of the nineteenth century belong in this period [*Aufklärung*]. These men . . . cannot be dismissed simply because they were called Aufklärung Catholics [*Aufklärer*]" (pp. 84 f.). Cf. below note 154, where the Catholic clergy of Baden praise the bishop of Württemberg for promoting "Aufklärung" in his diocese—in 1837.

[3]August Hagen, *Der Reformkatholizismus in der Diözese Rottenburg* (Stuttgart, 1962).

[4]Ernest Koenker, *The Liturgical Renaissance in the Roman Catholic Church* (Chicago, 1954), pp. 21 ff.; Trapp, *op. cit.*, pp. 357 ff.

[5]Olivier Rousseau, *The Progress of the Liturgy* (Westminster, Md., 1951), p. vii. The original French version was published in 1944.

[6]Perhaps the first outstanding exception to this view is to be found in the excellent work by Waldemar Trapp, *Vorgeschichte und Ursprung der liturgischen Bewegung* vorwiegend in Hinsicht auf das deutsche Sprachgebiet (Würzburg, Buchdruckerei Richard Mayr, 1939). Trapp has done an extraordinarily thorough research job into the liturgical reform efforts of the Aufklärung in Germany, and has been an invaluable assistance in the writing of this study. Moreover, he gives a sympathetic, balanced presentation of the positions of the Aufklärung Catholics, although some post-Vatican II Catholic scholars might think he darkens the shadows of the Aufklärung somewhat unduly because of pre-conciliar ecclestiastical pressures. It is of interest to note that Dom Rousseau's book mentioned above, which is very condemnatory of the Aufklärung, does not make use of this work of Trapp's, although it was published some five years before Rousseau's.

[7]Jansenism stemmed from the Fleming Cornelius Jansen, the bishop of Ypres, whose single major work, *Augustinus*, appeared in 1640, two years after his death; it was mainly a study of the question of grace in the teaching of St. Augustine. It tended toward a rigoristic position and soon became the source of a vigorous theological controversy, which also quickly took on political dimensions. Louis XIV of France wanted a unified nation behind him for his various military

adventures and hence attempted in various ways at different times to suppress the Jansenists. Doubtless part of the reason he opposed them was that they had become the champions of various religious reforms, and the virus of reform could spread too easily from the religious sphere to the political. The harrassing of Jansenists, which included severe psychical and physical punishment of the nuns of the convent of Port-Royal, reached a high point with the papal bull *Unigenitus*, issued at the urging of Louis XIV in 1713 against the writings of the Jansenist Pasquier Quesnel. In *Unigenitus* 101 statements culled from the writings of Quesnel so as to form a sort of summary of Jansenist teaching were condemned. The condemned statements included: "To snatch from the simple people this consolation of joining their voice to the voice of the whole Church is a custom contrary to the apostolic practice and to the intention of God. (Denz. 1436)"; "The reading of Sacred Scripture is for all. (Denz. 1430)"; (Cf. Vatican II Council *Dogmatic Constitution on Divine Revelation*, par. 22: "Easy access to sacred scripture should be provided for all the Christian faithful.") After the enforced acceptance of the bull *Unigenitus* the Jansenist influence was felt in many places for many decades afterwards. In sum it should be noted that Jansenism was a very complex phenomenon; "Popular speech confuses it with rigorism, with which it is connected only in an accidental way" (*New Catholic Encyclopedia*, article on Jansenism).

[8]Prosper Guéranger was born in France in 1805, became a priest and later a Benedictine monk and Abbot of Solesmes Abbey. He was a follower, for a while, of Lammenais in his ultramontanism, but broke with him when he ran into difficulties with Rome. Guéranger was a traditionalist and in general conservative and oriented toward authority. He re-founded Solesmes Abbey, from which Beuron Abbey in southwestern Germany was re-established and thence Maria Laach Abbey in the Mosel valley, all of which have been famous centers of liturgical renewal in the nineteenth and twentieth centuries. His most famous writings are the two multi-volume works *Institutions liturgiques*, 3 vols. (Le Mans et Paris, 1840/51); *Année liturgique*, 9 vols. (Le mans et Paris, 1841/66) [completion of vols. 10–15 by L. Fromage, Paris, 1878/1901]. He is often referred to as the father of the Liturgical Movement, as, for example, in Rousseau, *op. cit.*, p. 3: "The 'Liturgical Movement' with all its directives, ideals, and accomplishments, goes back to Dom Guéranger."

[9]In writing about Jansenism Sainte-Beuve referred to Guéranger's attitude toward Jansenism: "There is a curious chapter in Dom Guéranger's work where this entire effort to spread Christian doctrine and increase the spirit of prayer in the seventeenth century is presented as the result of a great conspiracy against the belief of the faithful"(C.A. Sainte-Beuve, *Port-Royal*, 5 vols. [Paris, 1840/61], vol. V, p. 233).

[10]Henri Bremond, *Histoire littéraire du sentiment religieux en France*, 11 vols. (Paris, 1932), esp. vols. IX and X. Cf. vol. X, pp. 38–39, where Bremond raises serious doubts concerning the value of Guéranger's scholarship and judgments on the liturgical reformers of the seventeenth and eighteenth centuries.

[11]*Ibid.*, p. 33. On page 34 Bremond says that in studying the Jansenist liturgical reformers of seventeenth-century France he must "resist the infinitely venerable authority and vehement seduction of Dom Guéranger." Moreover, he believes that the then recent liturgical reforms inaugurated by Pope Pius X were inspired by the same principles which inspired those Gallican liturgical reforms of the seventeenth century.

[12]*Le Bréviaire Romain en Latin et en Français*, 4 vols., 1680.

[13]*L'Année chrétienne* ou les messes des dimanches, féries et fêtes de toute l'année en latin et en français, avec l'explication des épîtres et des évangiles et un abrégé de la vie des saints, dont on fait l'office. [lst 6 vols., 1677–1686 (death of Letourneaux) others by Flammand Ruth d'Ans.]

[14]"The papal Nuncio one day said to P. de La Chaise that His Holiness demanded that . . . *l'Année chrétienne* be suppressed *because in it the Mass is translated into French* [italics added]." Saint-Beuve, *op. cit.*, vol. V, p. 221.

[15]Between 1587 and 1660 there were at least five translations of the ordinary of the Mass into French, 1587, 1607, 1616, 1618, 1651, the last one by Archbishop Harlay of Paris and acclaimed by the entire French episcopacy; there were also at least two translations of the complete Missal, 1651 and 1654, the last one being re-printed in 1655, only a generation before Letourneaux included his translation of the ordinary of the Mass in his l'Année chrétienne. Cf. Bremond, op. cit., vol. IX, pp. 182-183.

[16]Josef de Voisin, Le Missel romain, selon le réglement du concile de Trente, traduit en français, avec l'explication de toutes les messes, etc., 5 vols. (Paris, 1660). On January 12, 1661 Pope Alexander VII wrote: "It has come to our attention, and we perceive it with great sorrow, that in the kingdom of France certain sons of perdition, curious about novelites, which is dangerous to souls, and disdainful of the regulations and practice of the Church, have had the audacity to translate into French the Roman Missal, which until now has been written in Latin, following the usage approved for so long in the Church; once it was translated they had it put into print, thereby making it available to every person of whatever rank or sex. Thus they attempted by a temerious effort to cast down and trample the comprehensive majesty the Latin language was given to the sacrosanct rites and to expose the dignity of the divine mysteries to the vulgar crowd [vulgo] . . . . We abhor and detest this novelty which deforms the perpetual beauty of the Church and which easily engenders disobedience, temerity, audacity, sedition, schism, and many other evils. Therefore, by our own decision [motu proprio], with our own certain knowledge and mature deliberation, we damn, reprove, and interdict perpetually [perpetuo] the Missal already translated into French by anyone or which in the future might be translated and published by someone [ita Missale praefatum Gallico idiomate a quocumque conscriptum, vel in posterum alias quomodolibet conscribendum et evulgandum—for some reason Guéranger, when translating this papal letter into French in his Institutions liturgiques, vol. II, p. 13, translated this whole Latin phrase merely by saying the "above-mentioned Missal translated into French," and elsewhere did not translate the words perpetuo damnamus, although in another part of the volume he does give the full Latin text. Could it be that in the 1840's even Guéranger, who vigorously opposed the translation of the canon of the Mass into the vernacular, was embarassed by Alexander VII's condemning in such a totally unrestricted manner the translation of the Missal in general into French forever?] and we wish to be held damned, reproved and interdicted its printing, reading and retention by any and all faithful Christians of both sexes of whatever grade, order, condition, dignity, honor or preeminence, save that a special and individual permission might be had; we issue this prohibition in perpetuity under pain of excommunication incurred automatically, commanding that whoever should have such a Missal now, or in the future should in any manner obtain one, present it really and effectively and turn it over to the Ordinary or Inquisitor of the place, who, if there is no interposing custom, should consign it to the fire, being sure it is entirely burned, all objections by anyone notwithstanding. Given in Rome in St. Mary Major, under the seal of the Fisherman, January 12, 1661, the sixth year of our pontificate" (Latin text in Guéranger, Institutions liturgiques, vol. II, p. 118).

[17]Guéranger, Institutions liturgiques, vol. II, pp. 202f. The similarity, and even identity, of many of the things done by the Curé of Asnières with the post-Vatican II Mass is most striking.

[18]For the influence of Jansenism in Germany see W. Deinhardt, Der Jansenismus in deutschen Landen (München, 1929); in Austria, see Eduard Winter, Josephinismus (Berlin, 1962).

[19]Denz. 1533. Cf. Vatican II Council Constitution on the Sacred Liturgy, par. 34: "The rites should be distinguished by a noble simplicity; they should be short, clear, and unencumbered by useless repetitions; they should be within the people's powers of comprehension, and normally should not require much explanation." Cf. also par. 30: "By way of promoting active participation, the people should be encouraged to take part by means of acclamations, responses,

psalmody, antiphons, and songs, as well as by actions, gestures, and bodily attitudes." Note also that as a result of Vatican II and post-conciliar national conferences of bishops the Mass and sacraments were being celebrated in the vernacular all over the world by 1967.

[20]Denz. 1531.

[21]It should be noted that even before Vatican II Catholic scholarship had, very slowly, to be sure, begun to take a somewhat more balanced view of the reform efforts of Jansenism. For example, B. Matteucci, who is said to "have judged the Synod of Pistoia quite disparagingly," [Mario Rosa, "Italian Jansenism and the Synod of Pistoia," in *Historical Investigations*, vol. 17 of *Concilium* (New York, 1966) p. 36.] wrote in the *New Catholic Encyclopedia*, "Jansenistic Piety": "At the same time it did affirm certain real values, though sometimes in conflicting forms and manners: the historical sense of revelation, the living and genuine feeling of the liturgy, a profound sense of mastery, a simplicity of worship, a devout and liturgical reception of the Sacraments, a more popular participation in religious functions, a love for religious culture, and an austere style of Christian life. It advocated the direct study of the Scriptures and of patristic and conciliar tradition, a critical revision of the texts of faith and piety, reform in discipline and morals, and improvement in the theory and practice of religious formation. Not a few of the aspirations and movements of the 20th century were anticipated in Jansenism."

[22]Cf. Alexander Dru, *The Contribution of German Catholicism*, vol. 101 of *Twentieth Century Encyclopedia of Catholicism* (New York, 1963), p. 24. Perhaps two of the best examples of such Aufklärung Catholics were Karl Theodor von Dalberg, Archbishop and chief of state of various domains in Germany, and Ignaz Heinrich von Wessenberg, who was appointed by von Dalberg as his Vicar General for the diocese of Constance in southwestern Germany and northern Switzerland. Concerning the difference between the German and the Western European Enlightenment W. Maurer states: "One cannot distinguish sharply enough between the West European and German Enlightenment. A radical Aufklärung movement of large proportion never arose in Germany" (*Aufklärung, Idealismus und Restauration*, Giessen, 1930, p. 147).

[23]Cf., e.g., Franz Schnadel, *Deutsche Geschichte im Neunzehnten Jahrhundert*, vol. IV, (Freiburg, 1951, 2nd. ed.), pp. 50–62.

[24]Of course a later work need not necessarily be more "mature." The author might simply grow more conservative with age, or might become more susceptible to conservative pressures as he advanced in his career and had more to lose, or gain. For a similar opinion see Trapp, *op. cit.*, p. 204, note 77, also p. 230, note 245.

[25]Cf. August Hagen, *Die kirchliche Aufklärung in der Diözese Rottenburg* (Stuttgart, 1953), pp. 9–214. Werkmeister was born October 22, 1745, in Füssen in Bavaria, entered the Benedictine monastery of Neresheim in Allgäu in 1764, was ordained to the priesthood in 1769, became novice master and professor of philosophy both at his monastery and the Lyzeum in Freising in 1770, Court Preacher in Stuttgart in 1784, and in 1790 left the order, with papal permission. In 1796 he became pastor in Steinbach in Württemberg, and Chief Church Counsel in Stuttgart in 1817. He died on July 16, 1823.

[26]Cf. Trapp, *op. cit.,* pp. 19–68. Trapp divides Aufklärung Catholics into extreme and moderate representatives of the Aufklärung, although at times he notes it is difficult to decide where to place a man; even within the so-called extreme Aufklärung Catholics there is a wide variance in positions espoused.

[27]Cf. Hagen, *op. cit.*, pp. 29, 42–43, and elsewhere, where Hagen, a careful historian and a very orthodox pre-Vatican II Catholic theologian, rejects the claim that Werkmeister was a deist and severely criticizes Bishop Heinrich Brück, who repeatedly made the claim in his historical writings, for making statements beyond what his evidence would bear. On pages 147 and 148

Hagen is particularly severe in his criticism of the gullibility, and perhaps worse, of the Vatican Secretary of State, Cardinal Consalvi, and other curial and pro-curial persons who attacked Werkmeister by saying that he wished to eliminate the belief in the divinity of Christ. In a note written on September 2, 1817, by Consalvi to Wessenberg he was accused of conspiring with five other very evil priests, including Werkmeister, to obliterate the idea of the divinity of Christ in Germany within a period of two years, and that several of the most highly respected persons were prepared to substantiate this charge with authentic testimony and documents. Werkmeister was highly indignant and wrote: "For God's sake, you Romans! Can't you see . . . that the carrying out of such a plan, even if it could be hatched in the brain of a maniac, is absolutely impossible? Can't you feel it with your hands that through your gullibility you have been fobbed off with a fantastic lie? How could five or six men, even if they were as talented, energetic and zealous as they were wicked, entertain the fanatic thought of obliterating, in the short period of two years, from the minds of all Catholics in Germany such a deeply penetrated, such a holy and honored belief, as the belief in the divinity of Jesus. . . "(Hagen, *op. cit.*, p. 148).

[28]For a similar opinion cf. Sebastian Merkle, *Die katholische Beurteilung des Aufklärungszeitalters* (Berlin, 1909), pp. 29–30.

[29]Ignaz Heinrich von Wessenberg was born November 4, 1774, in Dresden, received a canonicat in Constance in 1797, was appointed Vicar General of Constance in 1802, ordained to the priesthood in 1812, after Dalberg's death in 1817 elected Chapter Vicar of Constance and, despite Rome's opposition, remained the diocesan administrator until 1827. From 1819 to 1833 he was a member of the Ständekammer of the Duchy of Baden. He died on August 9, 1860.

[30]Trapp gives further examples of other distorted generalizations about the Aufklärung. "The more one digs into the Aufklärung, the more one recognizes its many-sidedness, the more careful one is about generalized apodictic statements. While it is true that for an overall survey certain generalizations will have to be recognized as valid, nevertheless several current judgments are not only generalizations which always only partly and to a limited extent reflect reality, but rather are false and off the mark, particularly when they attempt to generalize about the extreme and moderate Aufklärung together. The charge is often made that the Aufklärung was unhistorical; in this connection the charge is certainly not correct. Many were well grounded in history, but for them it had more of the practical goal of providing a foundation for and strengthening their own concerns. Consequently the really strictly scientific research was less stressed" (Trapp, *op. cit.*, p. 67).

[31]*Ibid.*, pp. 19–21.

[32]Vitus Anton Winter was born May 22, 1750, near Landshut, was ordained to the priesthood in 1778, became Chief City Pastor in Ingolstadt and Professor of Church History and Pastoral Theology at the University there in 1794, and Pastor and Professor of Catechetics, Liturgics and Patrology in 1801 in Landshut after the Bavarian University moved from Ingolstadt to Landshut. Winter published several important works in liturgics and became the center of a school of liturgical reform. He died February 2, 1814.

[33]Vitus A. Winter, *Liturgie, was sie sein soll* (München, 1809), p. 173.

[34]Anton Josef Dorsch and Felix Anton Blau, *Beiträge zur Verbesserung des äusseren Gottesdienstes in der katholischen Kirche,* vol. I, part I (Frankfurt, 1789), p. 181 [published anonymously and originally planned as a periodical—see p. 80]. Anton Josef Dorsch was born in 1758 near Mainz, became a priest in 1781, Professor of Philosophy at the University of Mainz in 1784, and Professor of Moral Theology at the Episcopal Academy in Strassburg in 1791, from 1792 onward in French state service until his death in 1819. Felix Anton Blau was born in 1754 in Walldürn, became a Chaplain in Aschaffenburg in 1779, and in 1782 Professor of Philosophy, in 1784 Professor of Dogmatics, at the Episcopal University in Mainz and vice-rector of the seminary there. He participated in the French Revolution and died on December 23, 1798.

[35]Cf. Hermann Lauer, *Geschichte der katholischen Kirche in Baden* (Freiburg, 1908), p. 53. Even in the middle of the twentieth century priests and religious would jest by saying, "You lie like a second nocturne," referring to the readings on the lives of the saints in that part of Matins; for example, St. Nicholas was said to have been so saintly as an infant that he abstained from his mother's breast on Monday, Wednesday and Friday!

[36]"What is this frequent running back and forth of the priest and his ministers, this right, left, and about face, supposed to mean?" Johannes Anton Theiner, *Die katholische Kirche Schlesiens, dargestellt von einem katholischen Geistlichen* (Altenburg, 1826), p. 250. Similar attitudes were expressed by Vitus A. Winter, *Erstes deutsches kritisches Messbuch* (München, 1810), p. 324; Dorsch and Blau, *op. cit.*, p. 20; and Johann Baptist Graser, *Prüfung des katholisch praktischen Religiosunterrichtes von einem katholischen Religionslerher* (Leipzig, 1800), pp. 437 f. [anonymous]. Theiner was born on December 15, 1799, in Breslau, became a priest in 1823, and Professor of Exegesis and Pastoral Theology at the University in Breslau in 1824, then pastor in various places from 1830 to 1845, when he was suspended and went over to the German Catholicism sect. Graser was born July 11, 1766, in Eltmann in Unterfranken, became a priest, and in 1804 became the School Counsel in Bamberg, and the same in Bayreuth in 1810, was pensioned in 1825. He took an ever more extreme position and eventually married. He died on February 28, 1841.

[37]Vitus Anton Winter, *Erstes deutshces kritisches katholisches Ritual mit stetem Hinblick auf die Agenden der Protestanten* (Landshut, 1811), p. 31. Cf. also Winter, *Versuche zur Verbesserung der katholischen Liturgie.* Erster Versuch Prüfung des Wertes und Unwertes unserer liturgischen Bücher (München, 1804), p. 137 [anonymous]; and Winter, *Liturgie*, pp. 172 ff.

[38]Adolf Rösch, *Das religiöse Leben in Hohenzollern unter dem Einflüsse des Wessenbergianismus, 1800—1850* (Köln, 1908), p. 14. This theme was stipulated in 1804. In 1805 the subject was "The most beautiful and purposeful text for a Mass hymn for people on the land; The best German Vesper devotions." In 1808 it was "Collection of good Vesper hymns for Sundays and feastdays; Collection of acceptable litanies and other prayers for public prayer hours." And in 1810 it was "Plan for an improved Ritual for the diocese of Constance with proper consideration for the current order." *Ibid.*

[39]Trapp, *op. cit.*, p. 53, gives only two references to Theiner, *Kirche*, pp. 214 and 261, but he does not give the quotations, and one quotation from Werkmeister, which would seem to deny the doctrine; but Trapp goes on to say that from the context it is clear that the statement does not deny the doctrine.

[40]*Leitfaden für die in den k. k. Erblanden vorgeschriebenen deutschen Vorlesungen über die Pastoraltheologie*, 2 vols. (Wien, 1785); vol. II, p. 38. Franz Giftschütz was born April 10, 1748, in Vienna, became a priest and later Professor of Pastoral Theology in Vienna, and died on August 10, 1788. Trapp, *op. cit.*, p. 88, lists him as somewhere in the middle between the extreme and moderate Aufklärung.

[41]Dorsch and Blau, *Belträge*, p. 100.

[42]Theiner, *Kirche*, p. 288 [first italics added].

[43]Winter, *Erstes Ritual*, p. 62.

[44]Johann Baptist von Hirscher was born on January 20, 1788, in Altergarten by Ravensburg, was ordained to the priesthood in 1810, became Professor of Moral and Pastoral Theology in Tübingen in 1817, then Professor of Moral Theology in Freiburg from 1837 to 1863, a member of the Cathedral Chapter in 1839 and the Cathedral Dean in 1850. He died on September 4, 1865.

[45]"Uber einige Störungen in dem richtigen Verhältnisse des Kirchenthums zu dem Zwecke des Christenthums," in *Theologische Quartalschrift* (Tübingen), vol. V (1823), pp. 221, 392 [anonymous]. "Wie schnell muss dann das Sakrament ein Zauberakt werden. . . . Die Sakramente müssen so lange Zauberakte . . . sein und bleiben." The moderately progressive *Linzer Monatschrift*, vol. III (1805), p. 346, also emphasized that although the sacraments worked *ex opere operato*, it should not be understood as an act of magic but as something which demanded cooperation.

[46]Winter, *Erstes Messbuch*, p. 31 and p. 24. In 1808 Wessenberg also stated that the primary aim of the liturgy was moral edification [cf. Rösch, *op. cit.*, p. 67, and Lauer, *op. cit.*, p. 59]. Sailer says the same; cf. below, note 55. Early in his career Werkmeister stated in clipped fashion: "Public encouragement to virute is this: public worship of God." [*Beiträge*, ed. by Dorsch and Blau, p. 212.]

[47]Cf. Winter, *Erstes Messbuch*, pp. 1 ff., and Matthäus Fingerlos, *Wozu sind Geistliche da?* 2 vols. (Salzburg, 1801), *passim*, esp. vol. I, pp. 86, 151, 180, 236; vol. II, pp. 62, 147, 285, 314. (Fingerlos was born September 6, 1748, in Flatschbach, was ordained to the priesthood, became Rector of the seminary in Salzburg in 1787, City Pastor at Mühldorf am Inn in 1801, was Professor of Pastoral Theology and Director of the Georgianum in Landshut and died on December 11, 1817.) Among the Aufklärung critics of the rather grim Kantian morality was Johann Michael Sailer who wrote: "Oh how it chills me when I read an ice-cold hymn in which nothing beyond an ice-cold duty is coldly dealt with and forced into a similarly cold rhyme"(*Neue Beiträge zur Bildung des Geistlichen*, 2 vols. (München, 1809/11), vol. II, p. 124). Johann Michael Sailer was born November 17, 1741, in Aresing by Schroebenhausen, became a Jesuit in 1770, a priest in 1775, Professor of Pastoral Theology in Dilligen, removed on charges of *Aufklärerei* in 1794, became Professor of Pastoral Theology in Ingolstadt in 1799, a member of the Cathedral Chapter in Regensburg in 1821, and bishop there in 1829. He died on May 20, 1832.

[48]Giftschütz, *op. cit.*, vol. II, p. 36.

[49]Bernard Bolzano was born on October 5, 1781, in Prague, was ordained to the priesthood in 1805, became Professor of Religion at the University of Prague in 1805, was removed from his professorship in 1819 with charges of unorthodoxy, wrote and was the inspiration of reform Catholicism in the Austria Empire until his death on December 18, 1848.

[50]*Lehrbuch der Religionswissenschaft* (Sulzbach, 1834), vol. I, p. 236. It should be recalled that utilitarianism was at this time becoming popular, particularly in England under the influence of Jeremy Bentham, whose principle was: "the greatest good for the greatest number of people." This principle, though similar, was really much more individually and atomisticly conceived than Bolzano's, which took the community as such more seriously.

[51]Winter, *Liturgie*, pp. 67 f.

[52]*Ibid.*, pp. 70 f.

[53]*Ibid.*, p. 213.

[54]*Erstes Ritual*, p. 69.

[55]*Vorlesungen aus der Pastoraltheologie*, 3 vols. (München, 1788/89), vol. III, p. 81. In the second edition, 1794, Sailer gives a slightly revised definition of the goal of the liturgy: "General edification is the end [*Zweck*] of all devotional services, and immortal salvation is the common ultimate end [*Endzweck*]."

[56]*Glückseligkeitslehre aus Vernunftgründen mit Rücksicht auf das Christentum*, 2 vols. (München, 1787/91), vol. II, pp. 334 f.

[57]*Ibid.*, pp. 208 f.

[58]*Beiträge zur Bildung*, vol. II, p. 264. Sailer attempts to keep the values of the Aufklärung and reject its excesses by making a distinction between "*Aufklärung und Aufklärerei*," the latter being a derogatory derivative—like the distinction between science and scientism. Cf. *ibid.*, p. 307.

[59]Cf. Eduard Winter, *Josephinismus*, p. 210. Waldemar Trapp makes a similar generalization when he states: "Similarly inaccurate is the charge made against the moderate Aufklärung, namely that they advocated a pure moralism in the sense that it was completely religionless. The Catholic Aufklärung saw in the preaching of Christ the demand of morality as first and most important. Therefore for them the moral aspect naturally stood in the foreground, but it was always to some extent religiously oriented" (Trapp, *op. cit.*, p. 67). Aegidius Jais wrote: "the communal edification [note the stress on the community—many Aufklärung Catholics had a great concern for the community, contrary to the myth about them] of the listeners, or the fostering of their moral betterment *according to the spirit of the gospel* [italics added] is the final goal of the sermon" (*Bemerkungen über die Seelsorge besonders auf dem Lande* (Salzburg, 1817), p. 52). Aegidius Jais was born on March 17, 1750, in Mittenwald in Bavaria, became a Benedictine at Benediktbeuren in 1769, a priest in 1776, Professor of Moral and Pastoral Theology at the University of Salzburg in 1803, tutor at the house of the Grand Duke of Tuscany from 1806 to 1814. He died on December 4, 1822. See Trapp, *op. cit.*, p. 111 for further information. Cf. also the well-known church historian Sebastian Merkle, *Die katholische Beurteiling*, pp. 63–65, where he takes his Catholic colleagues to task for the many sweeping charges of insipid moralizing they made against the Catholic Aufklärung; he says that the stress on the practical moral aspect was a necessary reaction against the previous over-emphasis on an irrelevant, corrupted, scholastic dogmatism.

[60]Concerning Aufklärung Catholicism Waldemar Trapp said that "In general it is stressed that the sermon is very important" (*op. cit.*, p. 37).

[61]Cf. C. Nörber, "Wessenberg," in Wetzer and Welte's *Kirchenlexikon* (Freiburg, 1901, 2nd. ed.), col. 1345.

[62]*Jahrschrift für Theologie und Kirchenrecht der Katholiken* (Ulm), vol. II (1808/10), p. 429. Benedikt Peuger too stated that he thought the sermon was the most important thing. [Friedrich Zoepfl, *Benedikt Peuger (Poiger)*. Ein Beitrag zur Geschichte der kirchlichen Aufklärung (München, 1933), p. 58.] Benedikt Peuger was born on August 17, 1755, in Kössen Bez. Kitzbühel, became an Augustinian at the Chorherrnstift St. Zeno by Reichenhall, was ordained to the priesthood in 1778, served as professor and librarian at St. Zeno's and in 1781 became its Cloister Pastor, became Professor of Philosophy at the Lyzeum in Munich in 1791, from 1795 on was pastor of various churches, the last being in Munich, where he died on April 11, 1832.

[63]Cf. e.g., *Jahrschrift für Theologie*, vol. II, pp. 609–61. Italics added.

[64]Winter, *Liturgie*, pp. 70 f. Italics added. In the following quotation the sermon is placed not above the Eucharist, but on a par with it: "the Mass as well as the sermon and the other portions of divine worship must be considered only as means to foster virtue; a sermon is and can be no less effective in attaining this goal as the hearing of holy Mass." ["Uber die Ursachen der Vernachlässigung des öffentlichen Gottesdienstes," *Geistliche Monatschrift* mit besonderer Rücksicht auf das Bistum Konstanz (Meersburg), vol. I (1802), p. 114.]

[65]*Decree on the Missionary Activity of the Church*, in: *The Documents of Vatican II*, ed. by Walter Abbott (New York, 1966), p. 591.

[66]For example, Wolfgang Müller recently wrote of Wessenberg: "It is absolutely not so that for Wessenberg divine worship is essentially completed in the sermon. His concept of the Holy

Mass and its value was thoroughly conservative. It is noteworthy that he placed great value in having Holy Communion distributed *during* Mass; he recommended that even when a general reception of communion could not be expected at least several be encouraged to come forward to receive" ("Wessenberg in heutiger Sicht," *Zeitschrift für Schweizerische Kirchengeschichte*, vol. LVIII (1964), p. 298).

[67]"Eucharistica sacra nunquam sine sermone, qui populum de mysterio repraesentato erudiat, sacerdos celebrabit" (Franz Oberthür, *Idea biblica ecclesiae*, 6 vols. (Würzburg, 1790/1821), vol. II, p. 132). Franz Oberthür was born on August 6, 1745, in Würzburg, became a priest in 1769, Professor of Dogmatics in Würzburg in 1773, was pensioned in 1809, became a member of the Cathedral Chapter in 1821, and died on August 30, 1831. Trapp places him between the extreme and moderate Aufklärung, *op. cit.*, p. 43. Another example of an Aufklärung Catholic who worked to re-fuse the Eucharist and the sermon was Friderich Brenner, who stated: "For over a thousand years the sermon was bound closely within the celebration of the Mass and thereby formed a totality—now this connection exists only in the rubrics of the Missal." ["Nebeneinander-stellung der alten und neuen Zeit hinsichtlich der Messe," in: Friderich Brenner, *Geschichtliche Darstellung der Verrichtung und Ausspendung der Sakramente von Christus bis auf unsere Zeit*, 3 vols. (Bamberg and Würzburg, 1818, 20, 24), vol. III, p. 403.] (Friderich Brenner was born on January 10, 1784, in Bamberg, became a priest in 1817, Vice-rector of the Bamberg seminary in 1813, was Professor of Dogmatics there from 1820 to 1845, became a member of the Cathedral Chapter in 1821, and Cathedral Dean in 1844. He died on August 20, 1848.) The very language used by many Catholic scholars writing about Aufklärung Catholics, [*op. cit.*, vol. IV, p. 12], said that for them "preaching and teaching became more important than the Mass," implying that preaching was not a constituent element of the Mass. However, Vatican II corroborated the Aufklärung position in the *Constitution on the Sacred Liturgy:* "Since the sermon is part of the liturgical service . . ." (Abbott, *op. cit.*, p. 149); "The homily, therefore, is to be highly esteemed as part of the liturgy itself . . ." (p. 155); "The two parts, which, in a certain sense, go to make up the Mass, namely, the liturgy of the word and the Eucharistic liturgy, are so closely connected with each other that they form but one single act of worship" (pp. 156–57).

[68]"Bischöfl, Verordnung v. 5 Jänner 1803 über die Pflicht der Seelsorger, an Sonn-und gebothenen Festagen Predigt und Katechese zu halten," in: *Sammlung bischöfl. Hirtenbriefe und Verordnungen Sr. Hoheit des Durchlauchtigsten Fürsten-Primas des Rheinischen Bundes, Bishchofs zu Konstanz Von dem Jahre 1801 bis 1808*, vol. I, pp. 84–85. The first bishop of the diocese of Rottenburg, which included a sizeable portion of the former diocese of Constance, Johann Baptist von Keller, issued a regulation of worship services for his diocese in 1837 in which he stated in this regard: "The sermon must be joined with every celebration of the Mass on all Sundays and Holy Days of Obligation. It is not only that it is proper to the Mass liturgy and the most ancient ecclesiastical customs that the sermon be delivered during the Mass after the Gospel, . . . therefore, the sermon is to be held every time during the Mass" ("Die Allgemeine Gottesdienst-Ordnung für das Bisthum Rottenburg," *Der Katholik*, vol. LXXII, p. 111).

It is interesting to compare this 1803 order of Wessenberg's with a parallel text from Vatican II—one hundred and sixty years later: "The homily, therefore, is to be highly esteemed as part of the liturgy itself; in fact, at those Masses which are celebrated with the assistance of the people on Sundays and feasts of obligation, it should not be omitted except for a serious reason" (*Constitution on the Sacred Liturgy*, Abbot, *op. cit.*, p. 155).

[69]Cf. Rösch, *op. cit.*, p. 41. Despite that bit of civil pressure Wessenberg still had difficulty in getting complete compliance. On December 10, 1807, over four years later, in writing up the documents on his visitation to the chapter in Trochtelfingen, he felt it necessary to add a codicil urging compliance concerning the preaching at Sunday and feastday Masses regulations. And the matter did not end there in that area of the small state of Hohenzollern; two other villages in 1809 sent in petitions to the government asking to be relieved from the obligation of regular preaching

because the priest had to say Mass in another church as well, and in the same year Trochtelfingen obtained an order from the government lifting the preaching obligation. [Rösch, *op. cit.*, p. 42.]

[70]"Über die Ursachen der Vernachlässigung des öffentlichen Gottesdienstes," *Geistliche Monatschrift* (Meersburg), vol. I (1802), p. 197.

[71]Jais, *op. cit.*, p. 49.

[72]Johannes Theiner, *op. cit.*, p. 395. Cf. a similar position in Winter, *Erstes Messbuch*, pp. 69 f., and Jais, *op. cit.*, p. 124.

[73]Rösch, *op. cit.*, p. 41. Italics added.

[74]Cf. Müller, *op. cit.*, p. 298.

[75]Cf. *Theologisch praktische Monatschrift zunächst für Seelsorger* (Linz), vol. I (1809), pp. 76, 167, and vol. II (1809), p. 166.

[76]Cf. Trapp, *op. cit.*, p. 57.

[77]Cf. Beda Pracher, *Entwurf eines neuen Rituals von einer Gesellschaft katholischer Geistlichen des Bistums Konstanz* (Tübingen, 1806), pp. 14 f. [anonymous until second edition, in 1814, under the title *Entwurf eines neuen Ritual*]; also, Burchard Thiel, *Die Liturgik der Aufklärungszeit* (Breslau, 1926), p. 19. Note Wessenberg's decree of March 31, 1803: "an Sonn- und Feiertagen . . . jedesmal . . . dem anwesdenden Volk das Evangelium des Tages vorlesen . . ." ("Bischöfl. Zirkular v. 31. März 1803 wegen Abhaltung einer Homilie während der Frühmesse an Sonn- und gobothenen Festtagen," in: *Sammulung etc.* [for complete title see note 68], vol. I, pp. 140 ff.).

[78]Cf., for example, Zöpfel, *Peuger*, p. 58; and Josef Lauber, *Institutiones Theologiae pastoralis compendiosae*, 3 vols. (Brünn, 1780–81), vol. I, pp. 114 ff.; and Josef Lauber, *Praktische Anleitungen zum Seelsorgeramte oder Pastoraltheologie für wirkliche und künftige Seelsorger*, 3 vols. (Brünn, 1790), vol. I pp. 188 f.; Fr. X. Schmidt, *Predigten vor dem Landvolke, in einem ganzen Jahrgange nach den Sonn- und Feiertags Evangelien*, 2 vols. (München, 1818); and Jais, *op. cit.*, pp. 120 ff.; on p. 51 he wrote that "God's word, the Gospel, the Christian doctrines of belief and morality," are the proper subjects of sermons. Vatican II put its stamp of approval on this Aufklärung position too: "By means of the homily the mysteries of the faith and the guiding principles of the Christian life are expounded from the sacred text during the course of the liturgical year" (*Constitution on the Sacred Liturgy*, Abbott, *op. cit.*, p. 155).

[79]E.g., "Bischöfl. Zirkular v. 31. März 1803 wegen Abhaltung einer Homilie während der Frühmesse an Sonn- und gebothenen Festtagen," in: *Sammlung etc.*, vol. I, p. 140; and "Bischöfl. Ordinariatszirkular v. 4. März 1809, in Betreff der Homilie während den Frühmessen," in: *Sammlung etc.* (Konstanz, 1809 ff.), vol. II., p. 56. Sailer was another example of an Aufklärung Catholic who made regular use of the homily; he related how he would, if not every day at least several times a week, turn and face the people after the Gospel and explain its contents in a few words. (*Neue Beiträge zur Bildung des Geistlichen*, 2 vols. [München, 1809–11], vol. II, p. 280.) Bishop Keller's 1837 worship service regulation for the diocese of Rottenburg decreed the same: ". . . an early Mass should be said during which the Gospel of the Mass should be read in German and a homiletic explanation of it be given. . . . An explanation of the Gospel absolutely must be in every Sunday and Feastday Mass" (*Der Katholik*, vol. LXXII, pp. 117, 119. See note 68).

[80]*Ibid.* Wessenberg, however, thought the training of much of the clergy was so poor that in the Ordinariatszirkular of March 4, 1809, he recommended the breviary by Johann Thaddäus Antonius Dereser [*Deutsches Brevier für Stiftsdamen, Klosterfrauen und jeden guten Christen*, 4

vols. (Augsburg, 1792)] as a source for homily material, and even permitted the reading of the appropriate homily on the Gospel of the day from Dereser, who included homilies for each Sunday's Gospels. (Johann Thaddäus Antonius Dereser was born on February 3, 1755, in Fahr am Main, became a Carmelite in 1776, a priest in 1780, Professor of Exegesis in Bonn in 1783, Cathedral Preacher and Rector of the seminary in Strassburg, was condemned to death in 1794 because he refused to take the oath to the Civil Constitution of the Clergy, but after ten months in prison was freed by the death of Robespierre, became Professor in Heidelberg in 1799 and in 1806 went with the whole faculty to Freiburg, became a secular priest in 1802, City Pastor in Karlsruhe in 1810, taught dogma and exegesis, was in Breslau from 1815 on, became Cathedral Canon there, and died on June 16, 1827. For information on Dereser's Breviary see Rösch, *op. cit.*, pp. 23 f.) Wessenberg also included a question about the use of written manuscripts by the priests in their sermons in the questionnaire the Deans of the diocese had to fill out in their local visitations (decree of May 13, 1805): "An manuscriptos sermones et catecheses asservet?" [Cf. Rösch, *op. cit.*, p. 7.]

[81]An interesting example of Wessenberg's concern for the connection between preaching and the Bible developed the first year Wessenberg took over as Vicar General of the diocese of Constance. There was an "Exemplar Sermon" that was preached every Saturday in Trochtelfingen, and on December 2, 1802, he wrote that although "he did not wish to hinder the continuation of this sermon, still, along with the exemplars there must be connected a key moral Christian doctrine each time. Likewise, the life of the Blessed Virgin Mary can not be preached on every time because the sacred Scriptures do not give us a detailed account of the life of Mary, but rather only a few fragments." [Cf. Rösch, *op. cit.*, p. 42.]

[82]Cf. *supra*, note 19.

[83]Cf. Trapp, *op. cit.*, p. 28.

[84]Cf. Hock-Bidermann, *Der österreichische Staatsrat* (Wien, 1879), p. 510.

[85]Cf. Franz Dorfmann, *Ausgestaltung der Pastoraltheologie zur Universitätsdisziplin* (Wien and Leipzig, 1910), p. 162.

[86]Cf. Sebastian, *Die theologische Dienerschaft am Hofe Josephs II* (Wien, 1868), p. 430.

[87]Johann Josef Nepomuk Pehem, *Abhandlung von Einführung der Volkssprache in den öffentlichen Gottesdienst* (Wien, 1783), p. 105. It is interesting to note that almost identical language was used by Vitus Anton Winter who wrote that Latin has the effect of "making the listeners stand there like statues, which unfortunately we have too often observed"(*Erstes Ritual*, p. 30). (Johann Josef Nepomuk Pehem was born on April 8, 1740 in Stockach on Bodensee, became Professor of Canon Law at Innsbruck in 1771, and the same in Vienna in 1779, and died May 7, 1799.)

[88]Pehem, *op. cit.*, p. 43.

[89]Benedikt Peuger, *Anekdotenbuch für katholische Priester*, 4 vols. (Graz, 1787/89), vol. I, p. 176 and vol. II, p. 14.

[90]Cf. Dorsch and Blau, *op. cit.*, p. 22.

[91]Friderich Brenner, "Etwas über die Einführung der Muttersprache bei der Liturgie," *Theologische Zeitschrift* (Bamberg and Würzburg), vol. I (1809), pp. 276 ff.

[92]I Cor. 14: 19. Cf. [anonymous], *Gründe für und wider die Einführung der deutschen Liturgie in der katholischen Kirche Deutschlands* (Donauwörth, 1812), p. 9; and Brenner, *op. cit.*, p. 279.

[93][Anonymous], *Gründe*, p. 7.

[94]Brenner, *op. cit.*, p. 291.

[95]Cf. [anonymous], *Gründe*, p. 33.

[96]*Ibid.*, p. 6. Note again the emphasis on bringing the Bible to the people.

[97]*Ibid.*, p. 34.

[98]Theiner, *op. cit.*, p. 193.

[99]*Ibid.*, p. 194.

[100]Brenner, *op. cit.*, p. 306. On pp. 298–318 Brenner has a detailed discussion of the arguments for Latin, and their rebuttal.

[101][Anonymous], *Gründe*, p. 42.

[102]Cf. Johann Michael Sailer, *Neue Beiträge zur Bildung des Geistlichen*, 2 vols. (München, 1809/11), vol. II, pp. 81 f.

[103]Cf. Johann Michael Sailer, *Vorlesungen aus der Pastoraltheologie*, 3 vols. (München, 1811/12, 3rd ed. [1st ed. 1788/89], vol. III, p. 184.

[104]Sailer, *Bildung des Geistlichen*, vol. II, pp. 252 f.

[105]Franz Anton Staudenmaier was born on September 11, 1800, in Donzdorf in Württemberg, was ordained a priest in 1827, became Professor of Dogmatic Theology at the new theology faculty in Giessen in 1830, the same at the University of Freiburg in 1837, was named a member of the Cathedral Chapter in Freiburg in 1843, and on January 19, 1856, he died in Freiburg.

[106]Franz Anton Staudenmaier, *Die kirchliche Aufgabe der Gegenwart* (Freiburg, 1849), p. 178.

[107]Johann Adam Möhler was born on May 6, 1796, in Jgersheim bei Mergentheim in Württemberg, became a priest in 1819, in 1826 became extra-ordinary Professor and in 1828 ordinary Professor of Church History at the University of Tübingen, and the same at the University of Munich in 1835, and died on April 12, 1838, in Munich.

[108]Johann Adam Möhler [anonymous], book review "Lehrbuch des Kirchenrechts mit Berücksichtigung der neuesten Verhältnisse," in *Theologische Quartalschrift*, vol. V (1823), pp. 293–294.

[109]*Ibid.*, pp. 297–298.

[110]Johann Adam Möhler [anonymous], 'Etwas über Missionen, namentlich der katholischen Kirche," *Theologische Quartalschrift*, vol. VII (1825), pp. 624–626. It is interesting to note that Möhler, in saying what he thought ought to be done in this matter of the vernacular, referred to the *aufgeklärte Katholik* twice in these three pages. It is clear from this that, at that time at least, the terms "Aufklärung" and "Aufklärung Catholic" had no pejorative connotations, at least not in Möhler's mind. Cf. also earlier in the same volume, p. 286 [see above, note 108], where in a book review Möhler stated: "There is something about the use of one's own mother tongue that is unspeakably uplifting for the mind of man, when in the most solemn, beautiful and noble spirit of his being he is in immediate contact with Christ his savior, which is what should happen in the Mass. Just as in its utter uniqueness the mother tongue proceeds from our innermost being, so does it also comprehend our being at its most vital and inner level; in a totally special way its tones

flow into our souls and bring forth the most wonderful effects. In the chief moments of the Mass the priest and people must engage in the innermost effective exchange—and what will accomplish this if not the bond of language? Indeed, with it there opens up that which was closed and movements in the soul manifest themselves which are numbered among the authentic divine epiphanies in our earthly lives."

[111]Johann Baptist von Hirscher, *Missae genuinam notionem eruere eiusque celebrandae rectum methodum monstrare tentavit* (Tübingen, 1821). A German translation was published under the title: *Versuch den ursprünglichen Begriff der heiligen Messe zu entwickeln und die richtige Art und Weise ihrer Feier zu bezeichnen* (Baden, 1838), translated by R. F. Diebold.

[112]*Ibid.*, pp. 68 ff. He wrote: "Evidens pariter esse videtur, quod Missa apud Germanos latine celebrata sibi ipsi condradicat. . . . Quod exteram [Celebrans] linguam adhibeat, omnem Celebrantis et populi communionem impossibilem reddit" (pp. 70-71). In two separate articles published around the same time Hirscher reiterated his conviction that the liturgy ought to be celebrated in the vernacular. [Johann Baptist von Hirscher (anonymous), "Ehrerbietige Wünsche und Andeutungen in Bezug auf Verbesserungen in der katholischen Kirchenzucht, zunächst in Deutschland," *Theologische Quartalschrift* (Tübingen), vol. IV (1822), pp. 242 f.; and, Johann Baptist von Hirscher (anonymous), "Uber einige Störungen in dem richtigen Verhältnisse des Kirchenthums zu dem Zwecke des Crhistenthums," *Theologische Quartalschrift*, vol. V (1823), pp. 393 f., e.g., "Es kann demnach keine Kirche ihren Cult in einer den Gläubigen unbekannten Sprache feyern. Sie nimmt ihnen sonst mit der andern Hand, was sie denselben mit der einen zu spenden scheint."]

[113]Cf. *ibid.*, p. 92.

[114]Cf. *ibid.*, pp. 95 ff. and 105.

[115]Johann Baptist von Hirscher, *Erörterungen über die grossen religiösen Fragen der Gegenwart*, 3 vols. (Freiburg, 1846/47/55).

[116]Quoted in Johann Baptist von Hircher, *Sympathies of the Continent*, or Proposals For a New Reformation, trans. and intro. by Arthur C. Coxe (Oxford, 1852), p. 193, note d. This is a translation of *Die kirchlichen Zustände der Gegenwart* (Tübingen, 1849).

[117]*Ibid.*

[118]*Ibid.*, p. 192.

[119]*Ibid.*, p. 194.

[120]*Ibid.*, pp. 194-196.

[121]Anton Selmar was born on March 25, 1757, in Weihbiechel bei Landshut, became a priest in 1783, Pastor in Aibling in 1794, and in Berg bei Landshut in 1805, and died on October 10, 1821.

[122]Cf. Anton L. Mayer, "Liturgie, Aufklärung und Klassizismus," *Jahrbuch für Liturgiewissenschaft*, vol. IX (1930), p. 118.

[123]Anton Selmar, autobiographical article in: *Gelehrten- und Schriftstellerlexikon der katholischen Geistlichkeit Deutschlands und der Schweiz*, 3 vols., ed. by Franz Karl Felder and Franz Josef Waitzenegger (Landshut, 1817/22), vol. II, p. 335.

[124]Beda Pracher was born on June 24, 1750, in Hohenstein in Oberpfalz, became a Benedictine novice (under the direction of Werkmeister) in 1769, worked in the Württemberg school system,

became a secular priest and a pastor first in Drackenstein, and then in 1790 in Leinstetten, City Pastor in Stockach in Baden in 1809, Pastor in Schörzingen in 1810, and Vicar General Counsel in Rottenburg in 1817, and died in 1819.

[125]Beda Pracher, *Entwurf eines neuen Rituals von einer Gesellschaft katholischer Geistlichen des Bistums Konstanz* (Tübingen, 1806), [anonymous, but 2nd ed. in 1814 with the title *Entwurf eines neuen Rituals* was signed with Pracher's name].

[126]Cf. *ibid.*, p. 12.

[127]Cf. Johann Baptist Sägmüller, *Die kirchliche Aufklärung am Hofe des Herzogs Karl Eugen von Württemberg* (Freiburg, 1906), pp. 149 ff.

[128]Benedikt Maria Werkmeister, *Gottensveherungen in der Karwoche zum Gebrauch der herzoglich württembergischen katholischen Hofkapelle* (Stuttgart, 1784).

[129]Benedikt Maria Werkmeister, *Gesangbuch nebst angehängten öffentlichen Gebeten zum Gebrauch der katholischen Hofkapelle in Stuttgart* (Stuttgart, 1784).

[130]From the forward of *ibid.*

[131]Hagen, *op. cit.*, p. 30.

[132]Benedikt Maria Werkmeister, *Uber die deutschen Mess- und Abendmahlsanstalten in der katholischen Hofkapelle zu Stuttgart* (Ulm, 1787).

[133]Cf. *Ibid.*, pp. 31 ff.

[134]Benedikt Maria Werkmeister, *Beiträge zur Verbesserung der katholischen Liturgie in Deutschland* (Ulm, 1789); this was the only volume of a planned series that appeared.

[135]*Ibid.*, pp. 346 f.

[136]Cf. Sägmüller, *op. cit.*, pp. 48 ff.

[137]Cf. Müller, "Wessenberg in heutiger Sicht," p. 299.

[138]Cf. "Allgemeine Gottesdienstordnung für all Rheinischen Bundeslande des Bistums Konstanz vom 16. März 1809," *Sammlung* [see note 68], vol. II (erste Fortsetzung 1809), p. 50.

[139]*Christkatholisches Gesang- und Andachtsbuch zum Gebrauche bey der öffentlichen Gottesvehrung im Bisthum Konstanz*, ed. by das bischöfliche Ordinariat, 2 parts (Konstanz, 1812); for a further discussion of this and other German hymnbooks Wessenberg published see Trapp, *op. cit.*, pp. 148–151. Among other things Trapp, who is quite cautious, states, "no false ideas of the Aufklärung are contained in the hymnbook" (p. 150), and that "it is absolutely astounding how much of value and beauty and how much understanding for the liturgy there is in it" (p. 151). Trapp also points out that in 1809 Wessenberg edited *Deutsche Lieder* in Zürich, in 1808 *Hymnen für den katholischen Gottesdienst* in Constance, and in 1825 *Lieder und Hymnen zur Gottesverehrung des Christen* in Constance (p. 151).

[140]"An in sabbatis et profestis diebus habeantur vesperae? . . . An in lingua Germanica?" decree by Wessenberg on May 22, 1805, *Sammlung*, vol. I, p. 226.

[141]Cf. Müller, *op. cit.*, p. 300.

[142]Cf. I. H. von Wessenberg, *Pastoralarchiv 1811*, vol. II, (Konstanz), p. 143 ff.

[143]Cf. I. H. von Wessenberg, *Pastoralarchiv 1812*, vol. I, (Konstanz), pp. 102 ff.

[144]"Bischöfliche Zikular von 5. April 1805 in Betreff der Feldsegnungen bey den Oeschbittgängen," *Sammlung*, vol. I, pp. 180–198; and "Bischöfliche Verordnung vom 1. May 1806 wegen feyerlicher Abhaltung der Fronleichnams-Prozession," *Sammlung*, vol. I, pp. 198–215.

[145] *Ritual. Nach dem Geiste und den Anordnungen der katholischen Kirche oder praktische Anleitung für den katholischen Seelsorger zur erbaulichen und lehrreichen Verwaltung des liturgischen Amtes. Zugleich ein Erbauugsbuch für die Gläubigen* (Stuttgart and Tübingen, 1831).

[146]Cf. Rösch, *op. cit.*, p. 79.

[147] *Ibid.*

[148]Johann Baptist von Keller was born on May 16, 1774, in Salem, became City Pastor in Radolfzell in 1806, the same in Stuttgart in 1808, the Vicar General in Rottenburg in 1819, and the first Bishop of Rottenburg in 1828, and died on October 17, 1845.

[149]"Allgemeine Gottesdienstordnung für das Bistum Rottenburg," printed in *Der Katholik* (Mainz), vol. LXXII, pp. 105–140, 209–244, and vol. LXXIII, pp. 30–49, 137–148, with a very extensive, ultra-conservative commentary.

[150] *Ibid.*, vol. LXXIII, p. 111.

[151] *Ibid.*, p. 127.

[152] *Katholisches Gesang- und Gebetbuch zur Feier des öffentlichen Gottesdienstes im Bistum Rottenburg* (Stuttgart, 1838).

[153] *Der Katholik*, vol. LXXIII, pp. 44–45.

[154] *Badischen Kirchenblatt*, No. 45 (1838); also largely in the commentary on Keller's 1837 worship ordinance in *Der Katholik*, vol. LXXIII, pp. 155–158. The polarity of positions held among German Catholic clergy regarding the Aufklärung at that time is well exemplified on page 155 of that commentary where the anonymous author refers to the *Badischen Kirchenblatt* as an "un-catholic" and "un-churchly" paper, whereas the statement quoted from the Baden clergy begins by praising Bishop Keller for promoting an authentic "Aufklärung" in his diocese.

[155]See *supra*, notes 140 and 145.

[156] *Der Katholik*, vol. LXXIII, pp. 45–46. It is interesting to note that the conservatives who normally were very much in favor of the authority of the bishop, in this instance came out in support of the authority and orthodoxy of the laity over that of the clergy, or at least that part of the clergy with which the author disagreed. In this particular instance, of course, the author violently disagreed with the bishop as well. But through a distinction, which the author based on a convenient presupposition, the authority of bishop Keller was not quite totally rejected by the *Katholik*: "We must . . . view the Worship Service Regulation as a product which, in those parts to be rejected, was forced upon the bishop half by the deviant clergy and half by secular influences." *Der Katholik*, vol. LXXIII, p. 153.

[157] *Der Katholik*, vol. LXXIII, pp. 45–46. The moderately conservative Catholic church historian, Father August Hagen, in 1953 referred to the above commentary by *Der Katholik* as an "over-sharp" attack [Hagen, *op. cit.*, p. 248]. At least one progressive Catholic priest of the Rottenburg diocese responded vigorously to the attack by *Der Katholik*. Fridolin Huber referred to the critique "the most miserable product" ever to come out of the press [*Freimütige Blätter*, vol. II (1840), p. 147]. In this place Huber reviewed in detail the worship service regulation of the diocese of Rottenburg and supported it enthusiastically.

[158]Fridolin Huber was born on Otober 21, 1763, in Hochsaal bei Waldshut in Hauenstein, was ordained a priest in 1789, became parish administrator of Waldmössingen in 1796 and Pastor in 1799, and Pastor at Deisslingen bei Rottweil in 1809, Rector of the Rottenburg seminary from 1827 to 1828, and died on October 17, 1841.

[159]Fridolin Huber, *Wessenberg und das päpstliche Breve* (Tübingen, 1817), p. 45.

[160]Fridolin Huber, *Vollständige Beleuchtung der Denkschrift über das Verfahren des römischen Hofs bei der Ernennung des Generalvikars Frh. von Wessenberg zum Nachfolger im Bistum Konstanz und zu dessen Verwesung* (Rottweil, 1819), pp. 242 ff., 249, 251, 256.

[161]*Freimütige Blätter* (1840), part II, p. 205.

[162]*Kritisches Journal für das katholische Deutschland mit stäter Berücksichtigung der Felder-Mastiaux'schen Literatureitung* (Rottweil), vol. VI (1825), pp. 98 f.

[163]Fridolia Huber, *Verteidigung der katholischen Religion gegen die Angriffe unser Zeit* (Frankfurt, 1826), pp. 345 f.

[164]*Freimütige Blätter* (1838), part II, pp. 203 ff.

[165]This is an area of Catholic Church history that is almost entirely unknown, and which particularly today needs to be unearthed.

[166]*Freimütige Blätter* (1834), part II, pp. 60 ff., and (1836), part I, pp. 51 ff.

[167]See *supra*, note 116.

[168]Frantisek Nahlovsky (ed.) *Versammlung der Geistlichen, gehalten zu Prag am 18. und 22. Mai 1848* (Prag, 1848). See also the relatively favorable review of this book by the moderate Catholic theologian Sebastian Drey in the *Theologische Quartalschrift* (Tübingen) vol. XXX (1848), pp. 660–677; also, Winter, *op. cit.*, pp. 325–326.

[169]Cf. Lauer, *op. cit.*, p. 147.

[170]Rösch, *op. cit.*, pp. 74–75. It is interesting to note that in this instance of resistance by the clergy to liturgical change on the part of the diocesan chancery office is referred as a "loosened discipline" and "open contradiction and disobedience," whereas the resistance of the clergy to liturgical change promoted by Wessenberg was seen as a reflection of a true Catholic sense and orthodoxy, and therefore approved. [See above note 69.]

[171]Nörber, "Wessenberg" [see above note 61], col. 1373.

[172]One bit of contemporary evidence of this was given in ironic fashion by Josef Augustin Ginzel, Professor of Canon Law and Church History in Leitmeritz, Austria. Under a pseudonym Dr. Silvius he published the book *Über die Zukunft der Kirche in Österreich* (Regensburg bei Mainz, 1848), in which he vehemently attacked the reform program of Father Nahlovsky [see note 168], including the statement that "the struggle of the Church for a unified liturgical language rests on the nature of Christianity as a single way of salvation for all men of all nations and times." [Quoted in Winter, *op. cit.*, pp. 334 f.] However, in 1869, just before the beginning of Vatican I, he published another book, *Die Reform der Kirche*, in which he reversed almost all of his earlier positions, including "den Gebrauch der Landessprache in der Liturgie zuzulassen," [quoted in Winter, *op. cit.*, p. 335.], indicating, among other things, that the use of the vernacular was not then customary.

[173]Hircher, *Missae genuinam*, pp. 98 ff.

[174]Theiner, *op. cit.*, p. 279. In another place in the same work Theiner also stated: "The private Mass must also be changed. . . . Everything in the Mass must be thought of in terms of participation by the people. But the people do not take the least part in it, are neither instructed nor edified and the priest talks only with himself. In contradiction to the prayer formulary, 'Let us pray,' the priest prays to the people like, as it is said of Anthony of Padua, dumb fish" (*Ibid.*, p. 256 f.).

[175]E.g., Dorsch and Blau, *op. cit.*, p. 182.

[176]Benedikt Peuger, *Anekdotenbuch für katholische Priester,* 4 vols. (Graz, 1787/89), vol. II, pp. 82 ff.; and *Von Religionslehren* (Graz, 1788), pp. 10, 109; and *Religionspflichten* (Graz, 1789), pp. 309 ff.

[177]Beda Pracher, *Neue Liturgie des Pfarrers M. in K. Department L. der Nationalsynode zur Prüfung vorgelegt* (Tübingen, 1802), p. 35 [anonymous]. A similar attitude was also reflected in the writing of Johann Baptist von Hirscher when he frequently referred to the Mass as a love feast whereby the bond between God and the faithful and among the faithful themselves is strengthened and given a visible image. (Hirscher, "Ehrerbietige Wünsche und Andeutungen in Bezug auf Verbesserungen in der katholischen Kirchenzucht, zunächst in Deutschland," *Theologische Quartalschrift* (Tübingen), vol. IV (1822), pp. 248 f.) Wessenberg also expressed a similar idea when he referred to the Mass as having a double significance, namely, the celebration of the memorial of Christ and the meal of the Christian communal life together, which should waken and strengthen that new brotherly community among men whose life principle is love. (Beck, *op. cit.*, p. 128.)

[178]Franz Rieder, *Handbuch der k. k. Gesetze und Verordnungen über geistliche Angelegenheiten*, 3 vols. (Wien and Linz, 1847/59), vol. I (Wien, 2nd ed., 1848), p. 213. However, in a court decree from July 15, 1793, three years after the death of Emperor Joseph II and one year after the death of his brother and successor Leopold, the strictness of the previous rule was moderated to read: "so that in parish churches where several priests are present at most two masses may be said at the same time, namely one at the high altar and one at a side altar." Josef Kropatschek, *Sammlung der Gesetze, welche unter der glorreichen Regierung des Kaisers Franz II. in den sämtlichen k. k. Erblanden erschienen sind,* 15 vols. (Wien, 1973 ff.), vol. II, p. 455.

[179]Cf. A. Huhn, *Geschichte des Spitales der Kirche und der Pfarrei sum Hl. Geist in München* (München, 1893), pp. 300 ff.

[180]Wetzer and Welte, *Kirchenlexikon*, col. 1346; Lauer, *op. cit.*, p. 53.

[181]Frederich Brenner, *Geschichtliche Darstellung der Verrichtung und Ausspendung der Sakramente von Christus bis auf unsere Zeit*, 3 vols. (Bamberg and Würzburg, 1818/24), vol. III, p. 407.

[182]Hirscher, *Missae genuinam*, p. 87.

[183]*Der Katholik*, vol. LXXII, p. 119.

[184]*Ibid.*, p. 117. The conservative commentary in *Der Katholik* at this point is particularly strong: "This smells in general rather strongly of Pistoia. Does one wish with this and other such things perhaps to force traditional Catholic Christians [Altkatholische Christen] to listen to the sermons of unchurchly or rejected priests so as to spread the seed of the new light as broadly as possible—perhaps as in another land where the Catholic soldiers are commanded to attend Protestant sermons? This is a distorted means to promote attendance at the general parish Mass."

[185]Kropatschek, *op. cit.*, p. 504.

[186]"Uber die Ursachen der Vernachlässigung des öffentlichen Gottesdienstes," *Die Geistliche Monatschrift mit besonderer Rücksicht auf das Bistum Konstanz* (Meersburg), vol. I (1802), p. 50.

[187]Pracher, *Neue Liturgie*, pp. 28 f.; cf. Cölestin Wolfsgruber, *Christoph Anton Kardinal Migazzi Fürsterzbischof von Wien* (Ravensburg, 2nd ed. 1897), p. 710; Winter, *Versuche*, p. 156, and *Messbuch*, p. 436.

[188]Selmar Anton, *Die öffentlichen Gottesverehrungen der katholische Christen waren anfangs anders bescahffen als jetzt und sollten wieder anders werden, aus der Geschichte, Religion und Vernunft dargestellt* (Landshut, 1810), pp. 391, 618, 662.

[189]Brenner, *op. cit.*, vol. III, p. 321.

[190]Hirscher, *Missae genuinam*, p. 87.

[191]*Der Katholik*, vol. LXXII, p. 129.

[192]Benedikt Werkmeister, "Uber die katholische Messe," *Jahrschrift für Theologie und Kirchenrecht der Katholiken* (Ulm). vol. IV (1815/18), pp. 318 ff. Johann Baptist von Hirscher made almost the identical recommendation a few years later when he urged those priests who did not have a congregation to receive communion from the hands of the pastor or the bishop. [*Missae genuinam*, p. 87.]

[193]Lauer, *op. cit.*, p. 93. After Vatican II private masses largely disappeared; non-celebrating priests attend Mass in the congregation.

[194]Giftschütz, *op. cit.*, vol. II, p. 72.

[195]Winter, *Messbuch*, pp. 151 ff.

[196]Pracher, *Neue Liturgie*, p. 39.

[197]Hirscher, *Missae genuinam*, p. 80: "Nulli profecto festivae aut dominicali Missae communicantes deerunt."

[198]Hirscher, "Ehrerbietige Wünsche," pp. 248 ff.

[199]Wessenberg, *Ritual*, p. 117. See also the study of the liturgical undertakings of Wessenberg by Erwin Keller in a Beiheft of the *Freiburger Diözesanarchiv* (1964), Part I, chapter XI.

[200]Johann Adam Möhler, *Symbolik oder Darstellung der der dogmatischen Gegensätze der Katholiken und Protestanten* (Mainz, 1832; 10th ed. 1921), p. 249.

[201]Hirscher, "Ehererbietige Wünsche," p. 249.

[202]Johann Baptist von Hirscher, *Erörterungen über die grossen religiösen Fragen der Gegenwart*, 3 vols. (Freiburg, 1846, 47, 55), vol. II, p. 69.

[203]Ignaz Heinrich von Wessenberg, *Christkatholisches Gesang- und Andachtsbuch zum Gebrauch bey der öffentlichen Gottesverehrung im Bistum Konstanz* (Konstanz, 1812, 2nd ed. 1814), p. 414.

[204]Karl Schwarzel, *Anleitung zu einer vollständigen Pastoraltheologie*, 3 vols. (Augsburg, 1799/1800), vol. II, p. 191. A similar position was also expressed by Thomas Josef Powondra in his multi-volume work *Systema pastoralis*, 6 vols. (Wien, 1818/19), vol. V, pp. 91 f. Powondra was born on January 25, 1786, in Kremsier in Mähren, became a priest in 1810, Professor of Moral and Pastoral Theology at the Lyzeum in Linz in 1812, Professor of Pastoral Theology and

Liturgics at the Lyzeum in Olmütz in 1814, Dompropst at Trent in 1828, and died on March 27, 1832.

[205]Josef Lauber, *Institutiones Theologiae pastoralis compendiosae*, 3 vols. (Brünn, 1780/81, 2nd ed. Wien, 1782/83), vol. II, p. 203: "Ut hac ratione huius sacrificii unitas simul et universalitas magis indicetur, quae ratio non tam stricte valere videtur, si particulae adsint alio quovis die consecratae."

[206]*Ibid.*, pp. 207–209, which section is entitled "De frequenti communione suadenda vel dissuadenda."

[207]Powondra, *op. cit.*, vol. V, p. 120.

[208]Hirscher, "Ehrerbietige Wünsche," p. 254.

[209]Franz Xaver Schmid, *Liturgik der christ-katholischen Religione*, 3 vols. (Passau, 1832/33), vol. I, p. 620.

[210]Cf. Giftschütz, *op. cit.*, vol. II, p. 68; and Lauber, *op. cit.*, vol. II, p. 297.

[211]Schmid, *op. cit.*, vol. I, p. 612. Cf. Rösch, *op. cit.*, for some of the practices in part of Wessenberg's jurisdiction.

[212]Cf. for example Rösch, *op. cit.*, p. 113: "That the time of the Aufklärung introduced an absolutely wretched luke-warmness in the reception of the sacraments is well known."

[213]Winter, *Kritisches Ritual*, p. 184.

[214]Benedikt Werkmeister, "Über die katholische Messe," *Jahrschrift für Theologie und Kirchenrecht der Katholiken* (Ulm), vol. IV (1815/18), p. 304.

[215]Johannes Anton Theiner, *Der katholischen Kirche zweiter Teil*, oder Paragraphen zu einer neuen Verfassungsurkunde derselben (Altenburg, 1830), [anonymous], pp. 300/5.

[216]Hirscher, *Missae genuinam*, p. 106.

[217]Johann Baptist von Hirscher, *Erörterungen über die grossen religiösen Fragen der Gegenwart*, 3 vols. (Freiburg, 1846/55), vol. II (1846), p. 68.

[218]Johann Adam Möhler, review of *Harmonie der morgenländischen und abendländischen Kirche* by Hermann Joseph Schmitt in: *Theologische Quartalschrift* (Tübingen), vol. VI (1824), p. 649; e.g., "If the chalice will be generally permitted and someone believes he can express his reverence thereby . . . let him do so."

[219]*Ibid.*, pp. 648–9. "And when in order to prove that the priests alone had a right to the chalice the oh so wise scholastic theoligian Pullein said that the Apostles were priests, one might well dispose of the argument somewhat by noting that if the original custom were that only priests enjoyed the reception of the chalice, then also for twelve hundred years the laity must have been considered priests—that is if it were only so easy to dispose of habitual sophists."

[220]Johann Adam Möhler, review of *Die Kirchenagenden-Sache in dem preuschen Staate* by Ludwig Schaaf in: *Theologische Quartalschrift* (Tübingen), vol. VII (1825), p. 287-8. "When I with my whole soul transport myself to that hour wherein Jesus our savior . . . sat among his disciples and gave to all of them not only the blessed bread but also the cup out of which he drank . . . and then I remember that in our Church there are priests, even if they be only few, who say: I am a priest; the chalice belongs to me; I am extra-ordinary . . . then I can understand how the laity, indignant at such pride, such blasphemy . . . became derailed in their thinking and

separated themselves from those priests [the reference here is to the break of the Protestant Reformation] who do not know that the Lord said, whoever among you will become lord will have to become your servant. . . . It is said that this is merely something external; I say that the pride is not something external but rather something internal, and if the matter were something external and incidental then why, since it disturbs the devotion of so many, and certainly the outstanding priests most of all, is it allowed to annihilate unity and bring into the celebration of the most loving community an unholy division? Is the servant more than the lord?"

[221]Johann Adam Möhler, *Symbolik oder Darstellung der dogmatischen Gegensätze der Katholiken und Protestanten* (Mainz, 1832), p. 256.

[222]Cf. Wilhelm Bäumker, *Das katholische deutsche Kirchenlied in seinen Singweisen*, 4 vols. (Freiburg, 1891), vol. III, p. 11.

[223]Franz Rieder, *Handbuch der k. k. Gesetze und Verordnungen über geistliche Angelegenheiten*, 3 vols. (Wien and Linz, 1847/59), vol. I, p. 245.

[224]*Ibid.*, vol. III, p. 6.

[225]*Ibid.*, p. 13.

[226]Rupert Giessler, *Die geistliche Lieddictung der Katholiken im Zeitalter der Aufklärung* (Augsburg, 1928), p. 214. See also the remarks of the Aufklärung liturgist Aegidius Jais: "Well chosen church hymns sung by the majority of the congregation with devotion and vigor . . . are the oldest, most beautiful and most edifying church pieces" (Aegidius Jais, *Bemerkungen über die Seelsorge besonders auf dem Lande* (Salzburg, 1817), p. 261).

[227]Hagen, *op. cit.*, p. 27.

[228]*Ibid.*, pp. 27-28.

Was hilft es mir, ein Christ zu sein,
Wenn ich nicht christlich lebe.

And

Denn wer Deinen Willen weiss
Und ihn doch nicht tut mit Fleiss,
Der ist ärger als die Heiden
Und wird doppelt Streicht leiden.

See also Trapp, *op. cit.*, pp. 57–58.

[229]Cf. Bäumker, *op. cit.*, vol. III, p. 10; and Matthäus Schneiderwirth, *Das katholische Kirchenlied unter dem Einflüsse Gellerts und Klopstocks* (Münster, 1908), p. 42. The hymns of the Protestants J. K. Lavater, Christian F. Schubart, F. G. Klopstock and Christian F. Gellert were particularly drawn upon.

[230]Trapp, *op. cit.*, p. 206. The two books referred to by Trapp were by Johann Michael Sailer, *Vollständiges Lese- und Betbuch zum Gebrauch der Katholiken*, 2 vols. (München, 1783), and *Volständiges Gebetbuch für katholische Christen* (München, 1785). The hymns also found in the much used Ritual by Vitus Anton Winter, *Deutsches katholisches ausübendes Ritual*, 2 vols. (Frankfurt, 1813), and his Missal, *Erstes deutsches katholisches Messbuch* (München, 1810). were also mostly from Protestant authors.

[231]Werkmeister, *Jahrschrift*, vol. VI (1824/30), pp. 487 ff.

[232]Cf. *ibid.*, pp. 504 f. This introduction is reprinted in Bäumker, *op. cit.*, vol. III, pp. 146 ff.

[233]Cf. Hirscher, *Missae genuinam*, pp. 95 ff.; "Uber die Ursachen der Vernachlässigung des öffentlichen Gottesdienstes, *Die Geistliche Monatschrift*, vol. I (1802), p. 112; Frederich Brenner, "Etwas über die Einführung der Muttersprache bei der Liturgie," *Theologische Zeitschrift in Verbindung mit einer Gesellschaft Gelehrter*, vol. I (1809), p. 297.

[234]Cf. Hirscher, *Missae genuinam*, pp. 95 ff. Hirscher in the same place argued that the then customary manner of saying Mass, whereby the priest most often stood far from the people with his back turned toward them, merely fostered the division between the priest and the people, which was completely in contradiction to the primitive Church.

[235]Chronologically probably the nearest Catholic reformers who argued for having only one altar in a church were the members of the Synod of Pistoia; cf. Denzinger, 1531.

[236]Cf., for example, Frederich Brenner, "Nebeneinanderstellung der alten und neuen Zeit hinsichtlich der Messe," in: *Geschichtliche Darstellung der Verrichtung und Ausspendung der Sakramente von Christus bis auf unsere Zeiten*, 3 vols. (Bamberg and Würzburg, 118/24), vol. III, p. 408: "For nearly four hundred years each church contained only one altar, as a sign of Christian unity. Now every church is fitted out with several altars, to the disadvantage of the communal worship service."

[237]J. Schwertling, *Praktische Anwendung aller k. k. Verordnungen in geistlichen Sachen vom Antritt der Regierung Weiland Marien Theresien bis 1. Mai 1788* (Wien, 1788), vol. I, p. 126.

[238]Winter, *Erstes Messbuch*, pp. 322 f.

[239]*Ibid.*, p. 320; Brenner, *Geschichtliche Darstellung,* vol. III, p. 373; Hirscher, *Missae genuinam*, p. 105.

[240]Cf. Brenner, "Etwas über die Einführung," p. 297; Brenner, *Geschichtliche Darstellung*, vol. III, p. 373; Hirscher, *Missae genuinam*, p. 105.

[241]Winter, *Erstes Messbuch*, p. 320.

[242]*Ibid.*, p. 322; Lauber, *Institutiones*, vol. I, p. 29.

[243]Brenner, *Geschichtliche Darstellung*, vol. III, p. 408: "For a thousand years, outside of a cloth covering and here and there a cross the altar had absolutely no decorations. . . . At present the altars are overfilled with lights, flower pots, votive offerings, and relic containers so that the impact of such an image results in the irritation of many."

[244]In the post-Vatican II period it would be interesting to compare the current attitude toward church architecture with a description given of church architecture during the latter part of the eighteenth century in Austrian lands. "The main altar with the most blessed sacrament should be placed in the view of the faithful, and on the other hand the side altars ought to recede. Only on high feastdays may they be lit up and be the center of the Mass celebration. It is very instructive to visit such a Josephinist church. There are always some which have retained their character down to the present. They remind one of Protestant churches. The single altar has as its only decoration a large cross; for the rest of the walls are bare. The structure is simple and unpretentious. Everything which could deflect the senses from the main purpose of honoring God has been kept out of the church. The baroque style, which already by that time had become completely outmoded, had to also be overcome in the liturgy, so that this latter would again become accessible to the educated. It was into this battle that the emperor's decree against the baroque-styled churches was thrown. The numerous side altars, many with prie-dieus and offering boxes before the pictures and relics of favorite saints were to Joseph an abomination against which time and again inveighed with directives" (Edward Winter, *Josefinismus*, pp. 127–128).

245Trapp, *op. cit.*, p. 30, note 101.

246Vitus Anton Winter, *Erstes deutsches kritisches Messbuch* (München, 1810).

247Johann Baptist von Hirscher, *Missae genuinam notionem eruere eiusque celebrandae rectum methodum monstrare tentavit* (Tübingen, 1821). In 1823 it was placed on the Index, even though Hirscher had written it in Latin. Hirscher noted that he wrote it in Latin because it was directed toward scholars and churchmen, and not the common folk, and also that it would be more accessible to the proper people in foreign lands. [See above note 111.]

248*Ibid.*, pp. 108 ff. and 144 ff.

249*Ibid.*, pp. 95 ff.

250Cf. Benedikt Maria Werkmeister, *Gottesverehrungen in der Karwoche zum Gebrauche der H. W. K. Hofkapelle* (n. d., 1786), [anonymous], pp. 627 f.; and Werkmeister, *Beyträge zur Verbesserungen*, pp. 359 ff.

251Werkmeister, *Beyträge zur Verbesserungen*, p. 365.

252Pracher, *Entwurf eines neuen Rituals*, pp. 13, 20.

253*Ibid.*, pp. 12 f.

254Cf. Winter, *Messbuch*, pp. 288 f.; Anton Selmar, *Die öffentlichen Gottesverehrungen der katholischen Christen waren anfangs anders beschaffen als jetzt und sollten wieder anders werden, aus der Geschichte, Religion und Vernunft dargestellt* (Landshut, 1810), [anonymous], p. 663. Johann Michael Sailer also expressed himself in favor of revising the Missal, but he did so in a manner that disagreed rather significantly with the ideas of Winter, Werkmeister and others of a similar mind: "Cold reason . . . will find no firm connection between the fragments from the psalms and the ecclesiastical prayers, between the fragments from the Epistles and the fragments from the Gospels and will complain about this lack of unity." *Neue Beiträge zur Bildung des Geistlichen*, 2 vols. (München, 1809/11), vol. II, p. 191.

255Vitus Anton Winter, *Versuche zur Verbesserung der katholischen Liturgie. Erster Versuch Prüfung des Wertes und Unwertes unserer liturgischen Bücher* (München, 1804), [anonymous], p. 76.

256Hirscher, *Sympathies of the Continent*, pp. 209–10. As noted, this work of Hirscher's (the original German was *Die kirchlichen Zustände der Gegenwart*, Tübingen, 1849) was quickly put on the Index—in the latter part of 1849.

257Cf. *Freimütige Blätter* (1836), I, pp. 51 ff.; Hagen, *op. cit.*, p. 213; K. J. Huber, *Abendgespräche über die Mietmesse und andere kirchliche Gegenstände zur Fortsetzung der dringenden Vorstellung*, 3 vols. (Wien, 1784).

258Werkmeister, *Jahrschrift*, vol. II (1808/10), p. 204. See also Brenner, *Geschichtliche Darstellung*, vol. I, p. 305. Schmid, *Liturgik*, vol. I, pp. 169, 237.

259Brenner, *ibid.*, pp. 307. Brenner has some nine pages of similar criticisms of the then current administration of Baptism (vol. I, pp. 306–14).

260Johann Opstät, *Opera Theologica* (Venice, 1783), vol. V, p. 243; Theiner, *Kirche*, p. 313; Pracher, *Ritual*, pp. 281 ff.; Oberthür, *Idea Biblica*, vol. III, pp. 181–6; Winter, *Erstes Ritual*, pp. 167 ff.; Winter, *Ausübendes Ritual*, vol. I, pp. 139 ff.; Johann Baptist von Hirscher, *Ansichten von dem Jubiläum und unmassgebliche Andeutungen zu einer zweckmässigen Feier desselben* (Tübingen, 1826), *passim*; and Hirscher, *Missae genuinam*, p. 84.

[261]Hirscher, *ibid.*

[262]Freimütige Blätter (1836), I, p. 157.

[263]Beda Pracher, "Welche Mittel sind es vorzüglich, die der heilsamen Wirksamkeit der Bussanstalt nach den Pastoralerfahrungen Abbruch tun, und welche Mittel sind anzuwenden, um den wichtigen Zwech ihrer Einsetzung zu erreichen?" *Jahrschrift* (Ulm), vol. I (1807), p. 593.

[264]Dorsch and Blau, *op. cit.*, p. 165.

[265]Felix Anton Blau, "Uber das Beichtwesen in der kath. Kirche," in: Dorsch and Blau, *op. cit.*, p. 157.

[266]Winter and Fingerlos were two such Catholics who greatly treasured Confession but were concerned that it be used in a psychologically correct way so as to instruct and motivate the penitents. See Winter, *Erstes Ritual*, p. 126; Fingerlos, *Wozu sind Geistliche da*, vol. I, p. 289.

[267]*Der Katholik*, vol. LXXIII (1839), pp. 137–143.

[268]Winter, *Ausübendes Ritual*, vol. I, p. 100; F. X. Schmid, *Liturgik*, vol. I, p. 237.

[269]Cf. Pracher, *Neue Liturgie*, p. 83; Winter, *Erstes Ritual*, pp. 146 f.

[270]Brenner, *Geistliche Darstellung*, vol. 2, p. 247.

[271]Karl Schwarzel, *Versuch eines deutschen Rituals mit Beibehaltung des religiösen Altertums und Beisetzung einiger anpassenden neueren Verbesserungen* (Augsburg, 1809). Karl Schwarzel (also spelled Schwarzl) was born on February 19, 1746, at Eggendorf in Niederösterreich, became Professor of Dogmatics and Patrology at Innsbruck in 1779, Professor of Pastoral Theology at Freiburg in 1783, and also the Münsterpfarrer there in 1805, and died on March 4, 1809. Herenäus Haid was born on February 2, 1784, at Geisenfeld in Bavaria, became a priest in 1807, at Sailer's recommendation became Professor of Exegesis at the Seminary of St. Gallen in 1813, was appointed Cathedral Preacher in Munich in 1818 and in 1827 Cathedral Benefice (*Dombenefizist*), and died on January 7, 1873.

[272]*Einleitung in das Ritual nach dem Geist der katholischen Kirche* (München, 1812).

[273]Ludwig Busch was born on April 23, 1765, in Bamberg, became a pastor at Weismar a. M. in 1803, and at Schlesslitz in 1818, and died on July 30, 1822.

[274]Ludwig Busch, *Liturgischer Versuch oder deutsches Ritual für katholische Kirchen* (Erlangen, 1803).

[275]Beda Pracher, *Entwurf eines neuen Rituals von einer Gesellschaft katholischer Geistlichen des Bistums Konstanz* (Tübingen, 1806). [See above, note 77.] The second edition was no longer a Ritual in the usual sense; in addition to the rites of the Church it contained many private prayers and devotions and in some instances the prayers for blessings were really instructions and prayers for moral improvement. Cf. Hagen, *op. cit.*, p. 214.

[276]Benedikt Maria Werkmesiter, *Deutsches Ritual für kath. Seelsorger* (Freiburg and Konstanz, 1811).

[277]Anton Selmar, *Ritual für kath. Geistliche bei ihren Amtsverrichtungen* (München, 1812).

[278]Vitus Anton Winter, *Deutsches katholisches ausübendes Ritual*, 2 vols. (Frankfurt, 1813).

[279]Cf. Brück, *Geschichte der kath. Kirche in Deutschland im 19. Jh.*, vol. I, p. 461.

[280]Cf. *Breslauer Zeitschrift für katholische Theologie* (1832), 62/75.

[281]Cf. Trapp, *op. cit.*, p. 31.

[282]Ignaz Heinrich Karl von Wessenberg, *Ritual* Nach dem Geiste und den Anordnungen der katholischen Kirche, oder praktische Anleitung für den katholischen Seelsorger zur erbaulichen und lehrreichen Verwaltung des liturgischen Amtes. Zugleich ein Erbauungsbuch für die Gläubigen (Stuttgart and Tübingen, 1831, 2nd ed. 1833), [anonymous].

[283]*Ibid.*, p. iii.

[284]*Ibid.*, pp. i, ii.

[285]Rösch, *op. cit.*, p. 73. Fridolin Huber also was overjoyed at the publication of Wessenberg's Ritual. [*Freimütige Blätter* (1831), pp. 302 ff.]

[286]Trapp, *op. cit.*, pp. 152–53.

[287]*Rituale Friburgense* (Freiburg, 1835).

[288]Rösch, *op. cit.*, p. 71.

[289]*Ibid.*, p. 73.

[290]*Ibid.*, p. 74. On June 10, 1835, the Chapter at Haigerloch sent in the following request through a Deanery report: "Almost everyone has expressed himself in favor of requesting that alongside of the new Ritual that Ritual edited in Stuttgart and Tübingen [the Wessenberg Ritual], which has been in use also be allowed" (ibid.).

[291]*Ibid.*

[292]Johann Baptist Hirscher, "Einige Ansichten, betreffend die Vikariatsjahre der jungen Geistlichen," *Theologische Quartalschrift* (Tübingen), vol. X (1828), p. 50. Cf. also Fridolin Huber, *Antwort an die anonymischen Beurteiler der Schrift: Wessenberg und das päpstliche Breve* (Tübingen, 1818), p. 45: "However, even grant that the breviary were still very purposively, understandably and rationally structured; grant that all the fables were left out of it and everything were fully adapted to the circumstances of the one praying, it must of necessity gradually fall into a mechanical pattern."

[293]W. Mercy, *Über der Aufhebung der Klöster*, p. 12, quoted in Rösch, *op. cit.*, p. 35. Cf. also Trapp, *op. cit.* p. 60, where the author quotes several other eighteenth and nineteenth century Catholic theologians' criticisms of the legends of the saints in the breviary, e.g.: "The legends of the saints contained therein are often such that the saints themselves would not recognize themselves."

[294]A memorandum from the vicariate of the archbishopric of Mainz in 1789 stated that those priests in pastoral work ought to be obliged to read the Scriptures and perform other spiritual exercises rather than read the breviary, although for monasteries the breviary in a reformed version ought to be retained; reported in Georg Ludwig Karl Kopp, *Die katholische Kirche im neunzehnten Jahrhundert und die zeitgemässe Umgestaltung ihrer äusseren Verfassung* (Mainz, 1830), pp. 62 ff.

[295]Der Priester, der ein Weiser ist
Und eher sein Brevier als seines Bruders Not vergisst,
Der ist der Menschheit Zier.

Der Priester, der ein Dummkopf ist
Und bloss für das Brevier an seiner Kirche Krippe frisst,
Ist ein verworfenes Tier.

Quoted in Theiner, *op. cit.*, pp. 97 f.

[296]Cf. Winter, *Versuche zur Verbesserung*, pp. 129 ff.

[297]"Skizze einer Geschichte unseres Chorgesangs und Breviergebetes," *Jahrschrift für Theologie und Kirchenrecht der Katholiken* (Ulm), vol. II (1810), p. 437.

[298]Trapp, *op. cit.*, p. 41, noted that a great deal of the periodical literature of that time urged such changes.

[299]Cf. Guéranger, *Institutions liturgiques*, vol. II, pp. 165 ff.

[300]Cf. Trapp, *op. cit.*, p. 38.

[301]Cf. P. Volk, "Das Kölner Brevier von 1780," *Bonner Zeitschrift für Theologie und Seelsorge*, 3 (1926), pp. 88–91; and, Suitbert Bäumer, *Geschichte des Breviers* (Freiburg, 1895), pp. 539 ff.

[302]Kopp, *op. cit.*, p. 62; cf. note 285 above.

[303]Theiner, *op. cit.*, p. 98. Theiner noted that by then it was customary for many priests to no longer ask for dispensation from reciting the breviary, but to make their own judgments in the matter.

[304]Michl was from Ingolstadt and Brendel from Würzburg; cf. Rösch, *op. cit.*, pp. 31, 34.

[305]*Das Brevier von Louis Garson Dechant de la Paroisse de lunemonde* (Köln, 1779), pp. 42 ff.

[306]Franz Andreas Schramm, *Vollständiges System der Pastoraltheologie*, 2 vols. (Würzburg, 1788/91), vol. I, p. 83. Schramm was born on September 29, 1728, at Comorn, became a Jesuit, a Professor of Pastoral Theology at Budapest after the dissolution of the society, and died in Pressburg on March 9, 1810.

[307]Cf. Kopp, *op. cit.*, pp. 62 ff.

[308]Winter, *Versuche zur Verbesserung*, pp. 173 ff. He noted that it was improper that there was a more stringent obligation on reciting the breviary than on saying Mass, when the latter was much greater than the former.

[309]Rösch, *op. cit.*, p. 23; Rösch noted here that the "other works of devotion" most often was German Breviary by Dereser, discussed more in detail below.

[310]Quoted in *ibid.*, pp. 35–36. The chancery statement continued: "Also, we do not wish to burden anyone's conscience by specifying the choice of psalms, hymns, prayers or readings in the breviary, or by specifying the times of his prayer. . . ."

[311]Johann Thaddäus Antonius Dereser, *Deutsches Brevier für Stiftsdamen, Klosterfrauen und jeden guten Christen* Erbauungsbuch für all katholischen Christen auf alle Tage des Kirchenjahres, 4 vols. (Augsburg, 1792).

[312]For a biographical sketch of Dereser see n. 80.

[313]Dereser, *Deutsches Brevier*, Forward, p. ix.

[314]*Ibid.*

[315]*Jahrschrift für Theologie und Kirchenrecht der Katholiken* (Ulm), vol. V (1821), p. 188.

[316]Cf. Trapp, *op. cit.*, p. 32.

[317]*Archiv für Pastoralkonferenzen in den Landkapiteln des Bistums Konstanz* (Meersburg— later Freiburg), vol. II (1804), p. 385.

[318]Quoted in *Jahrschrift* (Ulm), vol. IV (1816), p. 243.

[319]*Ibid.*, vol. I (1806), p. 151.

[320]Cf. Rösch, *op. cit.*, p. 23; also n. 309.

[321]*Ibid.*, p. 35.

[322]Werkmeister, "Skizze einer Geschichte," p. 437.

[323]*Jahrschrift* (Ulm), vol. V (1821), p. 188.

[324]See note 310 above.

[325]Rösch, *op. cit.*, p. 36.

[326]*Rituale Augustanum* (Augsburg, 1764), pp. 363, 364, 374. Actually this Ritual is probably one of the earliest to show the beginnings of the influence of the Aufklärung. Trapp says of it: "it presents a compromise between the old and the Enlightenment orientation. The liturgical texts as compared to the earlier edition of 1688 was hardly changed at all. On the other hand there was an improvement and increase in the number of the rubrics. In these there was also a position taken against misuses and superstitions. The blessings were increased in number in order to drive out the many existing superstitious parabenedictions (Nebensegnungen)" (Trapp, *op. cit.*, p. 87).

[327]Franz Giftschütz, *Leitfaden für die in den k. u. k. Erblanden vorgeschriebenen Vorlesungen über die Pastoraltheologie*, 2 vols. (Wien, 1785).

[328]*Ibid.*, vol. II, p. 52.

[329]*Ibid.*, p. 62.

[330]*Ibid.*, p. 76.

[331]Whoever carried a *Lukaszettel* believed himself to be safe from all magic. One card taken from the breviary of a monk distinguished seven different uses for the *Lukaszettel*, including: "2. If such a card is placed in a soldered tin container and buried in the four corners of a garden or field, then storms and vermin can not harm the charmed person. . . . 5. These cards are helpful to pregnant women; if shortly before giving birth they swallow such a card the child will often bring the card with it into the world, either on the forehead . . . or in its little hand." Quoted in: Franz Andreas Schramm, *Vollständiges System der Pastorallehre*, 2 vols. (Würzburg, 1788/91), vol. I, pp. 574 ff.

[332]This was a statement made by Josef Weber, a natural science teacher at the high school in Dillingen, as quoted in: *ibid.*, p. 59.

[333]Trapp, *op. cit.*, p. 36. One cleric in the beginning of the nineteenth century wrote: "All pilgrimage churches and side chapels are very detrimental to the main worship service; they are a poison to morality, an opportunity for young people to shirk their duties and to disguise their

debaucheries and sins with the appearance of piety" (*Geistliche Monatschrift mit besonderer Rücksicht auf das Bistum Konstanz* (Meersburg, 1802), vol. I, p. 184).

[334]Theiner, *op. cit.*, pp. 356–378; Benedikt Peuger, *Anekdotenbuch für katholische Priester*, 4 vols. (Graz, 1787/89), vol. II, p. 206; Dorsch and Blau, *Beiträge*, p. 27.

[335]Lauber, *Institutiones*, vol. II, 2nd ed., p. 48 (his opposition is mild); Andre Reichenberger, *Pastoralanweisung* zum akademischen Gebrauch, 2 vols. (Wien, 1812), vol. II, pp. 213 ff. (This was a smaller version of an earlier five-volume work, which in 1814 was prescribed for use in all public and private theological schools in the Austrian Empire); Kopp, *op. cit.*, p. 236.

[336]In a decree issued in 1780. Cf. A. Gulielminetti, *Klemens Wenzeslaus, der letzte Fürstbischof von Augsburg und die religiöskirchliche Reformbewegung* (Neuburg a. D., 1911), pp. 15, 508–14.

[337]Georg Ludwig Karl Kopp, *Die katholische Kirche im neunzehnten Jahrhundert und die zeitgemässe Umgestaltung ihrer äusseren Verfassung (Mainz, 1830)*, p. 237.

[338]In a pastoral letter issued January 18, 1783. Cf. Kropatschek, *Handbuch*, vol. II, p. 410.

[339]Schnabel, *op. cit.*, p. 129.

[340]Trapp, *op. cit.*, p. 78. On the same page Trapp states: "A long line of other pastoral letters from that time are directed toward pastoral and liturgical questions. For example, those by J. M. v. Thun, Bishop of Gurk in 1750; H. v. Coloredo, Archbishop of Salzburg in 1782; J. Christian, Prince Bishop of Breslau in 1797; K. Th. Dalberg, Prince Bishop of Konztanz, etc. . . . It is specifically because of these pastoral letters that the bishops of that period are falsely condemned. The overwhelming majority of them were absolutely orthodox and of the best intentions."

[341]Quoted at length in: Rösch, *op. cit.*, pp. 93–94.

[342]Cf. *ibid.*, pp. 95 ff.

[343]Cf. *ibid.*, pp. 96 f.

[344]*Ibid.*, p. 97. "From about 1840 onwards an increase again becomes noticeable."

[345]Winter, *op. cit.*, p. 327.

[346]Wetzer and Welte, *op. cit.*, col. 1351.

[347]Fridolin Huber, *Freimütige Blätter*, vol. I (1834), p. 30.

[348]Fridolin Huber, *ibid.*, vol. II (1835), p. 193.

[349]Fridolin Huber, *Kritisches Journal für d. kath. Deutschland* (Rottweil), vol. VI (1825), p. 108.

[350]In speaking of Werkmeister, August Hagen stated: "Like most Aufklärung Catholics he took offense at the exaggeration in the cult of Mary and the saints during the baroque period, as is already indicated by the very title of his book: 'To the Immodest Devotees of the Saints, especially Mary' [*An die unbescheidenen Verehrer der Heiligen, besonders Mariä*], Hadamar, 1801. In Werkmeister's view the doctrine on the cult of the saints was lacking in beauty, purity, and simplicity because it had become overgrown with theological opinions, fanaticism, and ignorance" (Hagen, *op. cit.*, p. 89). See also, Peuger, *op. cit.*, vol. II, pp. 113 ff.; Frantisek Nahlovsky, *Versammlung der Geistlichen, gehalten zu Prag am 18. und 22. Mai 1848* (Prag, 1848)—note how late this is; Theiner, *Kirche*, p. 355. (Theiner here takes the extreme position of

the total elimination of the cult of the saints. Unlike most Aufklärung Catholics, Theiner became more radical with age.)

³⁵¹Cf. Gulielminetti, *op. cit.*, p. 44.

³⁵²Johann Baptist von Hirscher, "Über einige Störungen in dem richtigen Verhältnisse der Kirchentums zu dem Zwecke des Christentums," *Theologische Quartalschrift*, vol. VII (1823), p. 231. [Anonymous]

³⁵³Winter, *Erstes Messbuch*, pp. 170 f.

³⁵⁴Peuger, *Religionspflichten*, p. 166.

³⁵⁵Johann Michael Sailer, *Neue Beiträge zur Bildung der Geistlichen*, 2 vols. (München, 1809/11), vol. II, pp. 273 ff.

³⁵⁶Cf. Gulielminetti, *op. cit.*, p. 44.

³⁵⁷Sebastian Brunner, *Mysterien der Aufklärung in Osterreich* (Mainz, 1869), p. 151.

³⁵⁸*Der Katholik*, vol. LXXIII (1839), p. 33.

³⁵⁹Pracher, *Leitfaden*, p. 75.

³⁶⁰Philipp Josef Brunner was born on May 7, 1758, in Philipsburg, became pastor in Tiefenbach in 1787, a member of the Catholic Church Commission in Karlsruhe in 1803, and a member of the Catholic Church Section and likewise pastor in Hofweyer from 1813 to 1826, and died on November 4,1829.

³⁶¹Philipp Josef Brunner, *Neues Gebetbuch für aufgeklärte katholische Christen* (Heilbronn, 1801), pp. 345–360. The first edition was largely done by Werkmeister, even though Brunner was listed as editor. By 1832 it had gone through fourteen editions. Theiner wrote similarly: "Only with men is it necessary to turn to door keepers and good friends. God hears us without a middleman, without cost or expenditure" (*Kirche*, p. 363).

³⁶²Brunner, *ibid.*, p. 381.

³⁶³Werkmeister, *Unbescheidenen Verehrer*, p. 69.

³⁶⁴Brunner, *op. cit.*, p. 50.

³⁶⁵It might be noted that in his Ritual Beda Pracher retained a blessing of throats for the feast of St. Blaise, but the blessing did not refer in any way to St. Blaise. "Oh God, the candles, over which we call upon your name today, should become for us a visible image of the light with which we should always enlighten our understanding that we in deed may demonstrate that we are not beasts but creatures of reasons, and thereby never forget our human dignity." Pracher, *Ritual*, (2nd ed.), pp. 17 ff.

³⁶⁶Rösch, *op cit.*, p. 65.

³⁶⁷*Ibid.*, p. 81.

³⁶⁸For example, Conference theme number 137 from 1804 was expressed in this question: "Whence is the great predeliction of the people for the reduced feastdays, processions and pilgrimages? And how can this blind and unordered predeliction be moderated and directed to more important purposes?" [*Ibid.*]

369Schnabel, *op. cit.*, p. 129.

370Rösch, *op. cit.*, pp. 80, 82.

371Hirscher, *Sympathies of the Continent*, pp. 220–222.

372Benedikt Maria von Werkmeister, *An die unbescheidenen Verehrer der Heiligen, besonders Mariä* (Hadamar, 1801).

373Quoted in Trapp, *op. cit.*, p. 79.

374Rösch, *op. cit.*, p. 42.

375Benedikt Maria von Werkmeister, *Entwurf einer neuen Verfassung der deutschen katholischen Kirche in dem deutschen Staatenbund* (Karlsruhe, 1816), p. 88.

376Rösch, *op. cit.*, p. 41.

377Hirscher, *Sympathies of the Continent*, pp. 226–227; this is a quotation from Hirscher's *Erörterungen*, but quoted here in a footnote by the translator.

378Dorsch and Blau, *op. cit.*, p. 182.

379Peuger, *Anekdotenbuch*, vol. I, pp. 57 ff.

380Pracher, *Neue Liturgie*, p. 59.

381Pracher, *Leitfaden*, p. 76.

382Quoted in Rösch, *op. cit.*, p. 11.

383*Ibid.*, p. 12. Rösch described Haid's version of the Rosary as: "beginning with a preliminary meditation along with a verse of a hymn and a short prayer; then followed the Creed with a meditation on one of the articles; then five Hail Marys, with the five mysteries, are recited. After each Hail Mary there is a verse of a hymn and a short meditation on each mystery, after which a short prayer is added."

384*Ibid.* See also Peuger, *Anekdotenbuch*, vol. I, pp. 57 ff., where Peuger suggested that the Creed, Our Father and Hail Mary be recited only once and the priest should insert between the prayers his own pertinent prayers.

385Pracher even further adapted Haid's remodeled Rosary and printed it in his Ritual. *Ritual* (2nd ed.), pp. 74–106.

386*Ibid.*, p. 106.

387Cf. the Constitution on the Sacred Liturgy and the 24 post-conciliar liturgical reform documents found in Austin Flannery, ed., *Vatican Iouncil II* (Collegeville, Mn., 1975).

388Ignaz Heinrich von Wessenberg, "Allgemeiner Rezess über die Akten der Pastoralkonferenzen," *Archiv für Pastoralkonferenzen in den Landkapiteln des Bistums Konstanz* (Freiburg), vol. I (1827), pp. 4–28.

389"Dankadressen der Geistlichkeit des Bistums Konstanz an dessen Verweser beim Anlasse der neuen Diözesan-Einrichtung," *ibid.*, vol. II (1827), pp. 378–432.

390Hermann Lauer, *Geschichte der katholischen Kirche in Baden* (Freiburg, 1908), p. 63.

100 AUFKLÄRUNG CATHOLICISM

391Joseph Beck, *Freiherr I. Heinrich v. Wessenberg Sein Leben und Wirken* (Freiburg, 1862), pp. 103 ff.

392*Ibid.*, pp. 134 ff.

393Cf. Eduard Winter, *Bernard Bolzano und sein Kreis* (Leipzig, 1933).

394Joseph Schulte, "Hermes," *The Catholic Encyclopedia* (New York, 1910), vol. VII, p. 277.

395Eduard Winter, *Josephinismus* (Berlin, 1962), p. 273.

396Friedrich Lauchert, "Günther," *The Catholic Encyclopedia* (New York, 1910), vol. VII, p. 87.

397For a very antagonistic overview see Georg May, *Interkonfessionalismus in der ersten Hälfte des 19. Jahrhunderts* (Paderborn, 1969).

398*Ibid.*, pp. 42 ff.

399Hagen, *Kirchliche Aufklärung*, pp. 9 ff.

400Ferdinand Strobel, *Der Katholizismus und die liberalen Strömungen in Baden vor 1848* (Munich, 1938), pp. 106 f.

401*Ibid.*, pp. 102 f.

402*Ibid.*, pp. 117–19, 145–52.

403E. g., Johann Baptist von Hirscher, *Die kirchlichen Zustände der Gegenwart* (Tübingen, 1849).

404Strobel, *op. cit.*, pp. 73–81; Lauer, *op. cit.*, pp. 140–43.

405Lauer, *op. cit.*, p. 88.

406Michael Ott, "Constance," *The Catholic Encyclopedia* (New York, 1910), vol. IV, p. 287.

407Beck, *op. cit.*, pp. 94 f.

408Strobel, *op. cit.*, pp. 92 f.; cf. Trapp, *op. cit.*, pp. 19–21.

409*Ibid.*, p. 47; Strobel's reference is to Hermann Lauer, but no documentation is given at that point.

410*Ibid.*, pp. 47, 93.

411Lauer, *op. cit.*, pp. 94–96. The moderate conservative church historian August Hagen, *Geschichte der Diözese Rottenburg* (Stuttgart, 1956), p. 61, wrote: "How far the *Volk* were contaminated with the Aufklärung is difficult to say. The route would have been by way of the Aufklärung clergy and the Aufklärung publications. That communities in which such clergy worked for a long time fell under this spirit can be documented. The effect is to be traced to this very day. Certainly that did not include the majority of the communities of the diocese of Rottenburg. It is true that many catechisms of the Aufklärung were left untouched at that time, but the churchly catechisms held the upper hand—according to a survey from the year of 1841."

412Heinrich Maas, *Geschichte der katholischen Kirche im Grossherzogthum Baden* (Freiburg, 1891), pp. 153 ff.

[413]Strobel, *op. cit.*, pp. 86 f.

[414]*Ibid.*, pp. 18 f.

[415]*Mirari vos*, August 15, 1832, in *Acta Gregorii Papae* (Romae, 1901), vol. I, pp. 169–74. All citations here are taken from the English translation by Gregory Roettger in Colman J. Barry, ed., *Readings in Church History* (Westminster, MD: Newman, 1965), vol. III, p. 40.

[416]*Ibid.*, p. 38.

[417]*Ibid.*, p. 40.

[418]*Ibid.*, pp. 40 f.

[419]*Ibid.*, p. 41.

[420]*Ibid.*

[421]*Ibid.*, p. 74.

[422]Peter Stockmeier, "Congregation and Episcopal Office in the Ancient Church, *Bishops and People*, ed. and trans. by Leonard and Arlene Swidler (Philadelphia, 1970), pp. 71 ff.

[423]Leonard Swidler, "People, Priests, and Bishops in U.S. Catholic History," *ibid.*, p. 113 ff.

[424]*Ibid.*, p. 132.

[425]Leonard Swidler, *Freedom in the Church* (Dayton, 1969), pp. 136 f.